Barry Sheene, the 500c.c. world champion, astride a Suzuki G.S. 750 machine displayed at the Oulton Park Easter Monday race meeting by the Chester Suzuki Centre. Barry took the machine round a lap of the circuit. From left, Bob White, owner, Barry, Eric Pope, chief scrutineer of the

MOTOR CYCLE SCENE

JUMP JET
MAN AND
A LOTUS

There's c
somethi...
you

DEESI

NOW ON
FROM ALL NEWS

OBSERVER
FIRST WITH THE NEWS

R.I.G.P. LIMITED

Racing off the Page

WIDELINE

www.wideline.co.uk

Dedication

To Steff,
for patiently indulging my motorcycling passions,

and to Allen,
for enthusiastically fuelling them

Racing off the Page

John Moulton

Published and designed by **WIDELINE**   **www.wideline.co.uk**

A catalogue record for this book is available from the British Library

ISBN 978-1-8381336-5-8

Printed in the Czech Republic via Akcent Media Limited

FSC
www.fsc.org

MIX
Paper from
responsible sources
FSC® C014138

Credits. Photographs throughout were taken by John Moulton, with additional images supplied by Bob Edwards, Steff Moulton and the ever helpful Bill Snelling at www.ttracepics.com

Foreword

In May 1975 a nervous looking lad a few years younger than me arrived at Dugdale's motorbike shop to ask me about my plans for that year's TT. I'd been quite surprised to receive a request for an interview from a local newspaper. Usually the only interest they showed in bikes was when there was an accident, so I wasn't expecting much. Once he relaxed into his interview, John showed that he wasn't the run-of-the-mill cub-reporter however who covered jumble sales and the like, but rather an enthusiast, who had a knowledge of and a passion for motorbikes.

I discovered that, amazingly, John was writing a weekly column in the Cheshire Observer and before long that paper was sponsoring my great friend and benefactor, Allen Steele. When I attended a shakedown session for his BSA-powered outfit at Oulton Park there was John again, eagerly taking photographs and making notes for his column. Over the next few years, John seemed to be at every race meeting I attended. Although he was primarily there to write race reports for the paper, John had become friends with Allen and was his constant companion and helper. Later John went to work for my TT sponsor for 1977 and 1978, Heswall dealer Tom Loughridge, so our paths crossed even more often.

Through his weekly column, John promoted the positive side of motorcycling and gave local racers like myself much appreciated publicity. He also worked closely with the Chester Road Safety Office in running rider training courses for over fourteen years and John was, and still is, a great motorcycling enthusiast and ambassador. Like me, he was fortunate to work with bikes in the golden period of the 1970s and early 1980s and the tales in this book will bring back memories of those great times for those of us who were lucky enough to live through them.

Charlie Williams
Nine times TT winner

Prologue

In the summer of 1999, along with my friend of many years, Allen Steele, I was in the paddock at the famous Dundrod circuit in Northern Ireland, ready for the start of that year's Ulster Grand Prix. The last few days had been busy, with the hours being split between daytime preparation of the parade bikes and happy evenings reminiscing over a bottle of whisky or two.

One of the bikes was Allen's Yamaha TZ250H. Anyone who knows Allen will understand that most of the preparation had already been meticulously dealt with back in his workshop in Cheshire. As such we only had a few small tasks to complete, such as adjusting the tyre pressures and mixing the fuel. The other machine, an historically significant Yamaha FZ750, took rather more preparation. It was originally built for Sam McClements, for the 1985 Formula One TT. Unfortunately, on the night of 25th May 1985, it was lying at the bottom of Strangford Lough in an ex-fishing boat, alongside a number of Joey Dunlop's *intended* TT bikes.

As anyone who knows the story will be aware, the bikes were salvaged, though no one seriously thought they could be recommissioned, not least as the Yamaha had magnesium wheels which the sea water had rendered scrap. Somehow, through a great deal of hard work, favours called in and sheer determination, the story had a fairy tale ending; the bikes were miraculously rebuilt and McClements finished on the podium, in third place, behind Joey Dunlop and Tony Rutter. Back to 1999, here we were, getting the very same bike ready again for larger than life Irish race sponsor, Billy McKinstry, to ride in that year's parade. In fact, Billy had played a part in the original salvage job, so we had the story direct from the horse's mouth as only an Irishman could tell it. Our only problems were in recommissioning the long dormant carburettors and getting the damn thing going; though the bump starting problems may have been down to Billy's not inconsiderable weight. It was of no matter, the parade passed without incident and both Allen and Billy had an unforgettable time.

Back in the paddock, Allen and I got talking to another well set-up parader. His bike was parked next to his VW camper van and he was relaxing in a chair next to a cool bag full of beers. In no time at all, we were joining him for a welcome beer or two and it turned out that this hospitable man was none other than Terry Grotefield; a TT regular, riding for the famous Padgett racing dynasty among others, and a member of the legendary 1960s Continental Circus. Terry regaled us with tales from his racing days and, inevitably, Allen and I shared our own experiences with him. During the course of that late afternoon a variety of people passed by, gathered round, chatted and joined in. Joey Dunlop strolled over and talked for a while, though of his words of wisdom we were none the wiser. Most of the Irish lads nodded appreciably in all the appropriate places, but neither Allen nor I understood a word that Joey said. It was two nations divided by a common language.

Later that night, over a glass of whisky in Billy McKinstry's caravan, the conversation drifted back to the 1970s and how we had originally come to meet. A lot of water had passed under the bridge between then and now. Allen had enjoyed a successful sidecar racing career, Billy had a race team to his name and I had my own stories to tell. For a number of hectic years, I had written a weekly motorcycling column, road tested bikes for the press - including a couple of TT winners - worked in the motorbike trade and run a motorcycle training course. As we shared our memories, Allen said to me, *'We've certainly lived John and had a bloody good time. No one can take that away from us'*. He was right. We had both been lucky, to be involved with motorbikes and racing in the 1970s' golden days, but, thinking back, I reflected, *'Really, how did it all begin?'*

The late Tom Loughridge, to whom I owe so much

Chapter 1
From Steel to Paper

Working for the British Steel Corporation in 1973 wasn't all bad, even if the business was. Much of British manufacturing which British Steel supplied was on the slide and you didn't need to be a genius to spot which way the wind was blowing. I worked as an industrial buyer at the Shotton steel plant in North Wales and, despite making regular profits, Shotton didn't fit in with the Corporation's plans. It wasn't difficult to see that things were going to change, and not for the better. The changes were probably going to be catastrophic and as the workforce was around twelve thousand there was no way that all of us would be sticking around. I wanted to get out before there were major redundancies, while I still had a choice, the only problem being I had no idea what I could, or wanted, to do.

I started to look around and as luck would have it my dad's contacts came into play. One of his drinking buddies was the Circulation Manager at the local newspaper, the Cheshire Observer, and they had a vacancy for an assistant in his department. I had nothing to lose, so went for an interview and for some reason the Managing Director, Glyn Thomas, decided that he could better channel my talents through a different kind of job.

He thought I'd be suited to the role of Advertisement Representative, perhaps through some miscommunication over what an industrial buyer actually did? I guess the title implied I was used to wheeling and dealing – I wasn't – but what clinched the deal for me was the fact that I was offered the job on the spot. The money wasn't as good as I was currently getting, but there was the bonus of a company car and the security I no longer had. In truth I didn't really know what the job entailed, but there was nothing else on the horizon so I accepted it then and there. I was reluctant to leave Shotton, but I knew I was on a hiding to nothing if I stayed. Unfortunately, my pessimism was prophetic. The works still exists, part of Tata Steel, but I doubt more than a few I knew were ever able to hold on to their jobs.

My future was in the sale of advertising space, as that, I discovered, was what I would be doing. I was soon trying to convince local businesses to buy column inches and, though it was all new to me, it wasn't too difficult to learn and I soon picked up the skills. The daily routine wasn't too exacting either and while I can't say that I loved the job, I worked no harder than I had previously - and of course there was the company car. That was a real perk in 1973, but also a mixed blessing. I was obsessed with motorcycles and the Mini made my bike redundant for the daily commute. I was soon hardly riding, so I invested some time contemplating how I could spend more time legitimately messing around with bikes. My head was always buried in my weekly copy of Motor Cycle News, or the monthly Motorcycle Mechanics and it was probably the proliferation of such titles which sparked the idea which quite literally changed my life. Though a bit of context first.

Local newspapers scarcely exist today but pre-internet they were a hugely important source of local information; the national dailies simply couldn't compete. Remember, until 1960 the Guardian was the *Manchester* Guardian and papers such as the Yorkshire Evening Post sold over 250,000 copies a *day* at their height. That's more than national newspapers manage today. Additionally, in the 1970s local newspapers all seemed to have motoring correspondents, writing weekly columns about cars. Cars, but not to my knowledge, bikes. Indeed, few featured anything positive about motorcycles at all. Such things simply weren't heard of, as it was only a few years since the Daily Mirror had run their famous: *'Shock Issue: Suicide Squad'*, anti-motorcycle, front page.

Newsagents were awash with motorcycle publications however and sales were booming. I thought about it and came up with an obvious, but as far as I knew unique, suggestion, which I was naïve enough to present to my boss. I went to see Advertising Manager Eric White and asked, *'Why doesn't this newspaper have a motorcycling column?'* It was a simple question to which he mumbled a rather non-committal answer. So, I had the temerity to prod a bit further, suggesting that I could write one if he liked: *'Just an example of what one might look like'* and he clearly gave it some thought.

Eric may have known very little about motorbikes, indeed I knew he had no interest in them at all, but he was a canny businessman. I'm sure it must have been running around his mind that a motorcycling column might bring in additional advertising from local dealers as they were literally bursting at the seams around here. The local high streets were overrun with motorcycle shops so, to my amazement, he said, *'I'll have a word with the Editor'*, who was at the time Raymond Crabb. I can't remember if I was really expecting anything to come of this or not, but a few days later I was called into the Editor's office. He asked me to expand on my idea and, as Mr. Crabb clearly had more important things to do than to listen to my half-baked and perhaps long-winded plans, he just cut me off mid-sentence and said, *'Go away and write something and let me see it in a couple of days' time.'* So, with the confidence of youth and the qualification of a single 'O' Level in English Language, I set to, sat down and wrote.

Looking back, what I wrote was probably both pompous and over-ambitious. Essentially I listed what I, as a reader, would liked to have seen in a column. That is, something which would reflect and report on things nationally, but which would focus on local motorcycle events and personalities more i.e. the local *scene*. I wasn't total naïve; I hoped that the Editor would see the same potential as the Advertising Manager for additional advertising revenue, so my pièce de résistance was the claim that, *'The Observer would be the country's first local paper to have a regular motorcycling column.'* I didn't actually know if this was true, I still don't, but it was worth a punt and the Editor seemed to fall for it hook, line and sinker. A few days later, after he had read what I'd written, I was summoned back to his office where he grudgingly acknowledged that, if nothing else, I could write.

He quizzed me a little more about my ideas and, although he obviously had little understanding of the subject matter, he agreed that I could write a weekly column; or more precisely, a *trial* weekly column, which might be one week only if it bombed. As it happened Mr Crabb kept my test piece and I was surprised that it was this that appeared, verbatim, in the next edition of the paper, though not *quite* under my own name. It was decided that I would write under a nom-de-plume.

This sort of thing would soon be regarded as old fashioned, but many columnists still used an alias. I didn't really know why, I still don't, though perhaps it was so they could be easily replaced? Whatever, I thought long and hard about the issue before coming up with a simple and, I thought, elegant idea. I'd simply drop the 'M' from my surname; I'd become 'Oulton.' This way it wouldn't be too difficult for people I knew to guess who it really was writing, while it maintained a certain motorcycling ring. A local one to boot, as Oulton Park race track was only a few miles from the newspaper's offices. The Observer team all agreed it was neat, so Oulton it was, with a billboard poster being created using a photo of local racer and dealer Bill Smith. It was an image of him on board a racing Honda 750, a make with which he was synonymous, with the bold accompanying text declaring, 'Read Motorcycle Scene, by Oulton, every Friday in The Cheshire Observer.'

Motorcycle Scene wasn't the most inspired title for my column. It did what it said on the box however, and within a few days, as I drove around Chester, I started to see it emblazoned across posters all over the place. It filled me with a mixed sense of pride and panic as my bluff had been properly called. The column was go, but now I had to fill it. What had I done? In that initial column, I had optimistically written that I would like to feature road tests, but of course I hadn't really thought that one through. How might this happen? I had no idea how the glossy magazines approached it, so I visited each local dealer in turn, plying them with copies of the Observer featuring my initial Motorcycle Scene. In most cases I didn't need to introduce myself. The dealers already knew me, from my nose being stuck to their windows from my early teens, along with my many years of simply hanging around.

Others of course were more recently acquainted, through my touting for advertising sales. Either way, when I broached the subject of possible road test bikes familiarity didn't open any doors. There was little enthusiasm, which I shouldn't really have found surprising. I had no credentials as a journalist, no track record or back-catalogue of work to show, and motorcycles were literally selling themselves. I was endlessly giving out my contact details, but without a sniff of any takers. Would my new column take off at all?

By the autumn of '74 I still hadn't landed any test rides and knew that if I didn't get a few bikes soon I could easily run out of material, my credibility running out a long time beforehand. I could, and did, fill out my column with the local scrambles and grass track results, such as those from the Denbigh and Mold Motorcycle Club, along with local show reports, but I guess I was beginning to lose heart a bit. I was short of ideas when a friend, Mike Round, reminded me of one local dealer that I hadn't really considered before. It was a long-established Triumph dealership that had been owned by an old ex-destroyer captain, Len Williams. The business had recently changed hands and the new owner was a TT regular, Tom Loughridge. He had moved all the way up from the Midlands to take over and was obviously ambitious. He'd already obtained franchises for Honda, Suzuki, Yamaha and Laverda, which showed some serious intent. I thought it was worth a go, so took the short trip up, introducing myself to a man who would prove hugely influential on my life.

As a footnote, forty-five years later Charlie Williams contacted me, to help with the writing of Tom's obituary for Classic Racer magazine. It gave me time to reflect on the influence he had on me, on others, and more generally on motorcycle sport. Tom was an excellent, neat racer, with twenty-nine Isle of Man finishes to his name and a best of fifth place in the 1971 Production TT. But of greater importance to me was the fact that he'd go on to teach me every aspect of the motorcycle trade, demonstrating how you could have both a professional and ethical approach to motorcycle sales. I'd guess none of this from our first encounter however. On entering Tom Loughridge Motorcycles – for that was what it was now called - I was met by a wiry, amiable and animated Brummie who, in his excitement, seemed unable to stop talking about his new venture. It was clear he had huge expectations and a tour of the showrooms and workshop only reinforced the impression.

The type of diagnostic equipment which Tom Loughridge had in his shop in the early 1970s was unheard of at the time. Up until then you set your points with fag paper and tuned your carbs by ear as far as we were concerned

He hadn't been there long but you could see that he had already ploughed a huge amount of money into the business. The workshop contained thousands of pounds worth of special tools and looked more like an operating theatre than a garage. These were the days of black, oil-soaked, showroom floors – workshops were worse - dirty brown storemens' coats and old wooden trestles, if shops had any work benches at all. Tom's shop was several notches up. I was impressed and, eventually getting a word in edgeways – this guy really could talk - I explained my role at the paper, probably embellishing somewhat and inflating my status along the way. Why not? I was thinking, *'This might be my last shot?'* I ran copies of my most recent columns past him and, hoping that he'd not noticed the lack of any road tests, as confidently and professionally as possible, I asked, *'Would there be any chance of borrowing one of your bikes, to test?'*

I'm sure that I held my breath during the long silence that followed. Tumbleweed metaphorically blew down the street, but I needn't have worried. Tom was just mulling over the logistics, there was no reason to sweat, *'The Guardian have got my Laverda 750 until the weekend. But you can pick that up on the Saturday after and keep it for a week, if you like?'* 'Struth! Of course I liked. I'd fallen on my feet. I was even happier when Tom said that he would pay for an advert in the paper, to accompany any road-test report. I was a real life road-tester and just one rung down from the Guardian by the sounds of it. As back then, while most of the daily broadsheets didn't really cover motorcycles, the Guardian was more progressive than most; partly I suppose as the motorcycle industry was a political hot potato at the time, with NVT – Norton Villiers Triumph – Wedgie Benn and the Triumph Workers' Cooperative rarely off the front page.

You can imagine how I felt as I rushed back to the office. I was all set to announce my coup when Assistant Advertising Manager Bob Edwards swooped in to steal my thunder. He'd discovered that Sports Motorcycles of Manchester - later to be famously involved with Mike Hailwood's TT comeback - were holding a test day at Oulton Park and he had arranged for me to ride one of the new Norton Commando 850s: the Mk II A Interstate to be precise. London buses sprang to mind: two bikes at once after the drought, though as I was already anxious about the Laverda the prospect of riding the Norton, observed on a race track, put the pressure up by several bar.

I'd watched racing at Oulton Park before, but I'd never actually been on the track, any track. Be that as it may, a few days later, Bob drove me to my local Cheshire circuit for my baptism of fire. For this I at least looked semi-professional. I was wearing my brother's borrowed one-piece Lewis Leathers and a new-fangled full-face helmet, the latter still being a bit of a novelty among the open-faced alternatives and pudding basins you still saw around. I looked the part, so I felt half the job was done as I joined the long queue of riders in the paddock waiting for their turn. I hadn't realised that this was actually a public test day and that anyone could apply for a ride, but I was far from disheartened. I was actually relieved. I was just one among many and could preserve my anonymity, hide my lack of experience and my obvious nerves. That was until Bob, having considerably more self-confidence and front than me, went straight to the organisers, pulled rank, and arranged for the *'professional road tester'* to jump the queue. The power of the press hey! I really could have done without it.

The test day had been set up purely and simply to promote the latest version of the Commando. There were no other models available to ride, but in truth Norton, as part of NVT, had little else to flog anyway. These were the dying embers of the British motorcycle industry on show, but Norton still had about twenty Commandos available for the great unwashed to thrash. The number was diminishing however and the sight of a crashed Norton, being brought back to the paddock on a low-loader, was sobering just before I set off. It did little to improve my confidence as suddenly here I was, inexperienced cub-reporter, trundling around the track behind the bars of the most powerful motorcycle I'd ever ridden.

As I rode round, *'Do I really belong here?'* sorts of thoughts were running through my head, but the engine sounded beautiful and I quickly realised that the Commando was actually a cracking *learner* machine. The engine delivered the sort of torque which made the gearbox redundant, and while that's one of the worst journalistic clichés you can ever use, it was also true. It was a cliché that I was happy to let slip on paper, as the engine was a godsend. Otherwise, I was struggling to come to terms with the bike whilst at the same time trying to avoid faster riders. Many of these were clearly more accustomed to the power and handling available, as well as being familiar with Oulton Park. Within a few laps I was starting to get a hang of the layout, speeding up, though I never did get to grips with Old Hall Corner, the right-hander immediately after the start-finish straight. It didn't seem to matter what line I took, I still took it slower than others. Conversely the less rapid, tricky, tighter corners, such as Lodge at the end of the lap, suited me better and I took them quicker than most. By the time I was waved in at the end of the session, I was actually enjoying myself and had done enough to push the Commando a bit too. That was important. By 1974 the Norton was effectively an antique and many potential buyers would have doubted its potential. The basic engine dated back to 1947 or thereabouts, so it was really a bit of an anachronism by the 1970s, what with its separate gearbox, right-side gear lever and total absence of an electric start.

Despite my novice status and initial hesitation, the Commando had impressed me however, with its smoothness and torque, which challenged my preconceptions about its dated design. Its slightly old fashioned looks - black, with gold pin-striping – also belied the fact that the chassis was quite cutting-edge. The smoothness came from some clever and unique rubber *'Isolastic'* engine mounting, which isolated the rider from the rumbles down below, while retaining the ability to turn quickly and effortlessly. It was no mean feat for a bike of its size, especially since much of Norton's reputation had been built on the *featherbed* frame which had preceded the Commando's. I was surprised, as well as relieved at what was running round my brain. I had plenty to write about in my next article; I wouldn't be lost for words.

My review appeared in the next edition of the paper and I don't think my readers – *my* readers now please note - would have realised my lack of ability to do the Norton journalistic justice. My riding experience gave me nothing to compare it with though again, as a bit of background, that wasn't actually a prerequisite. BIKE had come out in 1971 and was the first magazine to really carry out comparison tests. That is back-to-back tests of similar machines. This gave prospective buyers the chance to compare different bikes, like for like. It was still a relatively new idea in the press and of course not universally popular with the manufacturers. They were used to a rather more charitable testing regime, with its roots dating back to the 1950s and '60s. Manufacturers were certainly not used to being marked against one another though, because of the Laverda promise, my chance to do exactly that came the following weekend.

On Saturday I was in Heswall to pick up the Laverda from Tom Loughridge. The bike was already sitting outside the showroom when I arrived and, as I'd never seen one in the flesh before, two things struck me immediately: its beautiful looks and the sheer size of the bloody thing. It was huge. It seemed massive compared to the Commando I'd just ridden so I was less worried about riding it than simply getting it off its centre-stand. This not least since Tom, during his pre-flight briefing, pointed out that this was actually his own machine, not a test model: as they'd say today, '*No pressure there then.*'

The Laverda was a 750SF2 and interesting as the '*SF*' referred to '*Super Freni*', the Italian for super brakes. The previous model had an impressive looking – if not so impressively performing – twin leading-shoe front drum brake. The SF2 had double discs at the front-end instead and looked even more impressive. Twin-discs were very much state of the art and probably necessary on the Laverda as, while the bike produced a similar 60bhp to the Commando, it was heavier, by nearly 100lbs.

Back outside, Tom showed me the controls which included a button for an electric starter, the pressing of which had the big twin bursting into life, very loudly. The starter also had the bike dancing around on its centre-stand, such were the levels of tick-over vibration. Despite the 750's gorgeous looks, this was unnerving. I wasn't at all sure I'd like the Laverda, but nervously I heaved the bike off its centre-stand, didn't drop it and climbed aboard. Determined not to stall the engine, I really concentrated as I engaged first gear and let out the clutch. It was heavy but I needn't have worried about fluffing it. The amount of torque available from tick-over was impressive and, once underway, I found that the Laverda wasn't too difficult to ride, apart from that wooden clutch, which persisted throughout. The bike was very long however, requiring considerable rider input to change direction quickly, though the upside was amazing stability on long, fast bends. The SF750 was already a favourite among continental endurance racers for this very same reason and a week later I was thankful for the Laverda's sure-footedness. I hit a patch of diesel as I accelerated from a slip road onto the M6: the bike slewed sideways but was back in line in an instant. There was no input from me, I was a mere passenger, I didn't even have time to think.

My conclusion? Overall, compared to the Commando, the amount of vibration that reached the rider was quite noticeable. It was normal for a time before balancer shafts however and nothing worked loose or

Tom Loughridge in his prime, racing his T500 Suzuki to fifth place at the TT in 1971

fell off during the test. The *Super Freni* really were progressive and powerful, even if I found the suspension rather too firm. That's another cliché, but it was true of all Italian bikes at the time. As I was to find out, Japanese bikes got you where you wanted to go comfortably; Italian bikes got you there fast.

As a fledgling tester it had been massively helpful for me to ride two ostensibly similar motorbikes; it made comparisons so much easier. The Norton was smoother, lighter, had a better clutch and was a more svelte and agile machine. The Laverda on the other hand was generally more sophisticated, had better brakes and was unflappably stable. The build quality of the Laverda was impressive too, and, while a desirable bike, the Commando was a relatively common sight on the road in comparison; the Laverda was pure exotica. Most motorcyclists would never have seen one in the flesh and my test model looked like a sculpture, hewn from solid. The Norton would have got the vote of many riders – it did, it massively outsold the Laverda – but for me, the character of the Italian machine shone through. In this regard these tests were a real eye opener. Had anyone asked me in advance what my dream bike was, I would have answered, *'Norton Commando'* without hesitation. These two rides taught me an important lesson. You learn a thousand times more about a bike through just ten minutes riding than reading everything that has ever been written about it. Despite its foibles, the Laverda was the one that would have got my money. Not that I had any of course. This made its return the following Saturday rather reluctant, though there was a silver lining: Tom seemed genuinely interested in my opinion.

Thankfully, as with the Commando, I was able to be very positive about its attributes, truthfully. The truthful bit was important, as I'd already thought through every tester's dilemma, *'What do you say if a bike is bloody awful?'* especially if a shop or manufacturer is paying to advertise. With the Laverda, it wasn't an issue. With my time aboard the Italian twin still fresh in my mind, it was easy to write a glowing report which appeared alongside Tom's advert. I thought it looked great so that same morning I took some copies over to Tom's shop, where he seemed equally impressed. That was a relief, but the biggest result was that Tom said that he could sort out more bikes for me to sample. *'Bingo!'* I was in. It looked as if my weekly column was a runner, even if the timing of these first tests wasn't exactly ideal. We were heading into winter. It would be spring before I could really get in some meaningful test rides, but this gave me time to develop a sideline.

Outside of work I had my own bikes. Up until now, I had owned a mixture of British parallel twins, from BSA and Triumph, a Yamaha 200 two-stroke twin and an East German 250 MZ two-stroke single. Plus, of course, the inevitable BSA Bantam; *everyone* of my generation had a BSA Bantam at some point. A Bantam was a rite of passage, but by the time I joined the Observer, I owned a Triumph Daytona, which was that firm's twin-carburettor sports 500. It was built alongside the slightly more famous 650cc models until some time in 1972 when the smaller twins were discontinued. It was still a relatively recent model,

My first two road test columns. The Norton Commando 850 and the Laverda 750. The print is too small to read in these images, but that might be intentional. These were my first attempts at 'real' journalism and my style may not have withstood the tests of time

but an under-used one. I was using the company car daily for my job, and needed to, so the Triumph was being neglected. I only really rode it at weekends, which made owning a high performance twin hard to justify; money was tight. I still wanted to ride however, so I started a round of the local dealers, looking for inspiration and something more economical to buy.

That's how, for the very first time, I bought a bike solely on its looks. In retrospect it proved an inspired impulse buy too. I walked into Westminster Motorcycles in Brook Street, Chester and there I came across an entirely new model to me: a Yamaha DT125. I was instantly intrigued by its cobby looks - there you go, another journalistic cliché - and its beautiful blue pinstriped tank. The upswept black exhaust, braced handlebars and trail tyres all looked really purposeful and when I sat on the little two-stroke single it immediately felt right. I knew next to nothing about the model, nor trail bikes in general, but decided there and then to buy it. Now, having just stepped off a 750 Laverda, you might be thinking, *'Why is this guy buying an off-road tiddler?'* Well the truth is I couldn't afford to run anything bigger and I also had this rather rosy outlook. I was getting free test bikes now, so why buy a bog standard street bike? I was going to be lent bikes like that for free. I wasn't disappointed with the Yamaha. It was fun to ride from the word go. It was light and responsive and, while it had little power compared to the lusty Triumph, in fairness it was brand new and not yet run in. Best of all I really liked the bike's upright riding position - I have done ever since – though I had little idea how to fully enjoy it.

I was a trail bike owner with no trail riding experience. As such, I joined the TRF (Trail Riders Fellowship), got the contact details of Pete Smith, their local rep, and told him my story. He invited me to his home and recommended a number of O.S. (Ordnance Survey) maps to bring. A few days later, armed as instructed, I rode the little Yamaha over and was greeted at the door by a tall dark man of about thirty five. He had close-cropped black hair, unusual for the time, and a strong Scouse accent and for some reason reminded me of a merchant seaman, just back from a long voyage out at sea. Pete had a cursory glance at my bike and then asked me to come in. Although he didn't say anything, I realised that Pete was not impressed by my Yamaha; he was a British bike man, through and through, and I discovered that he used a Triumph twin for his green lane riding. Despite this, Pete and I had a good evening and he was meticulous when marking my maps. Showing me places where I could legally ride, he explained that *'green lanes'* were unmade roads that could be legally used by motor vehicles and that there was a network of them all over England and Wales, *if* you knew where to find them. At the time, they were marked on O.S. maps as RUPPS (Roads Used as Public Paths) and Pete taught me how to identify them. I should note that the Rights of Way situation has changed a great deal since the 1970s and that many lanes that were legal to use then have now been re-categorised as off-limits; we had the best of it.

In addition to marking my maps and teaching me the basics of Rights of Way, Pete gave me a lot more to mull over that evening. We discussed bike preparation, pre-GPS navigation and courtesy towards others. Critically, Pete advised that in order to get better traction on unmade surfaces I would need to lower my tyre pressures when I went off tarmac. He also strongly recommended that I fitted security bolts to my wheel rims. This was to stop the tubes moving in the tyres, which was possible with the lower tyre pressures; it reduced the possibility of punctures. It was all stuff you can get off the internet today, but it was black arts to my generation.

I mustn't have made too bad of an impression on Pete as, when I was about to leave, he told me that he was in the process of starting a club – what would become the North Wales Green Lane Riders - and asked if I would like to join. His idea was to have a number of club runs, along with a monthly social night, though as yet he hadn't found a suitable venue. I was up for that and added that I could try to find a pub that would welcome us. Dad had plenty of contacts within the North Wales trade as he was a big darts player and ran a number of local football teams. We didn't see much of him when he wasn't at work to be honest, he was always out organising things, so I was confident that something could be arranged. Pete was pleased about that so we shook hands and I headed home, happy to have had such a positive evening and knowing what to do next. Within the week, the bike's rims had been fitted with security bolts, I'd bought a portable foot pump and I was prepared for my first attempt at going off-road.

That was the following Saturday, when I rode west from Chester into Wales, heading out on the Mold to Denbigh road, looking for a minor turn-off that would take me to my first green lane. I found it without too much difficulty, but would have missed the insignificant looking muddy track off to the right after two hundred yards had Pete not marked it on my map. I wouldn't have given it a second glance otherwise, but pulled over, deflated the tyres to about 12psi front and 10psi rear and rode gingerly up this muddy track in second gear. Instinctively I stood up. This initially felt strange to someone who'd only ever ridden firmly sitting down, but also totally natural. The DT felt similarly natural off-road and never had any misgivings, responding well, particularly as I remembered Pete's advice to leave the brakes well alone and to steer on the throttle.

My ascent probably never topped 15mph, but it still felt a great achievement. I took a moment at the top to catch my breath, as it was a lot harder work than I had thought, but I had to put my feet down anyway, to stop, to consult my map. Pete had marked the end of this lane as a T-junction and I could see that I now joined a fairly smooth flat track which went to the left, so I turned that way too, riding on, still standing, reaching third gear and 30mph's dizzy heights. Reaching the end of this track, I then turned around and retraced my steps, the muddy lane being more challenging as I was descending. Here I had to curb my natural instincts to flirt with the front brake. Even a light

The type of machine most favoured when I took up trail riding. A Triumph 500cc Adventurer twin, here on one of our later club runs in Wales, in March 1977. Smaller two-strokes would rapidly take over so my little DT125 was simply ahead of its time

application could have seen the front wheel locking, and me ruining my Yamaha's good looks. To anyone used to road riding the front brake is always the first port of call. If I wanted to keep off-roading, I'd have to re-learn all I knew, using the back brake as my main one or using no brake at all. And I did want to keep off-roading. The last forty minutes had been as much fun as I'd ever experienced on a bike; I couldn't wait to do more and I had good news for Pete too when I next saw him. I, or rather my dad, had found a suitable venue for our first meeting: the White Lion at Pulford near Chester, for which we set a date for our inaugural, sit-down, social.

The next green lane that I tried became one of my all-time favourites. It was known as '*The Wayfarer*', the pen name of Walter MacGregor Robinson, an enthusiastic cyclist from Liverpool who, in the decades between the Wars, rode far and wide across North Wales, recording his routes and experiences principally for Cycling magazine. A memorial stone to him was erected on the track near Llanarmon, in the Ceiriog Valley south of Llangollen and the ride to the start was about thirty miles from my home, via Wrexham and Glyn Ceiriog. Main roads were never the DT's forte but after Wrexham they became smaller and quieter, ideal for the 125. I easily found the start of the track - Pete's map marking was always excellent - but this one was to prove more challenging than the first.

For the first mile or so it climbed up a rocky stream bed. I had to pick my way slowly, choosing a path carefully between largely unseen rocks, but even so I fell off a couple of times, luckily at walking pace. Heaven alone knows how W. M. Robinson made it up here on a bone-shaker push-bike, but he evidently did, as at the top of the climb I found the plaque to '*Wayfarer*' and near it a large stone which had obviously been regularly disturbed. Out of curiosity I moved it myself and found a metal box underneath, inside of which was a book. It had been signed by many previous travellers and, as there was luckily a pen inside, I recorded my visit too, leaving everything as I had found it. The memorial was in such a beautiful location that I sat on a rock for about ten minutes, enjoying the view of the hills and the solitude, musing that this wasn't the sort of thing non-bikers would associate with a motorcycle ride. Communing with nature, or however else you want to describe it, the visceral connection to the elements that only riding a motorcycle provides. The track onwards, westwards towards Llandrillo was grassy and relatively easy to negotiate. It gave me a further chance to take in the view and, when I eventually reached tarmac again and I stopped to re-inflate my tyres, I realised I'd lost all track of time. I'd probably been on the *Wayfarer* for no more than an hour and a half, but all the same I'd not seen a living soul the entire time, my only company having been some sheep and spiralling buzzards overhead. I'd had another fantastic ride, but during these early ventures off-road one thing bothered me: Pete Smith's advice to always ride with someone else.

So far I had not heeded it, but the feeling of isolation on my last ride set me thinking. An accident miles from anywhere could have life-threatening consequences; remember, this was long before mobile phones and it could have taken days for someone to find me. These areas were pretty remote and rarely frequented by hill walkers. I had partially covered myself by leaving details of my planned route at home, but I knew that this wasn't enough so decided to tackle the problem in a different and, as it proved, a not very successful way, by taking a pillion passenger. I know what you're thinking, *'This doesn't sound very sensible'* .... and it wasn't.

Firstly I persuaded my friend Mike Round, the guy who had guided me to Tom Loughridge's shop. We rode to the *Wayfarer* again, with Mike on his BSA 500 Royal Star. My plan was to leave his bike at the point where I adjusted my tyres, ride two-up to the summit, turn around and ride back down again. Simple. It didn't take long for me to realise that I couldn't really stand up with poor old Mike on the back however, nor that a passenger badly affected the balance. The weight was all at the back and we were going uphill. The front-end was incredibly light, to a dangerous extent, while Mike's bulk sapped what little power the DT had. We eventually made it, but we spent more time on the floor than off. The fact that Mike was still speaking to me at the end of the day spoke volumes about the strength of our friendship. Sometime later I took my brother David on the back on a slightly less challenging run. We were actually doing quite well initially, until I crested a rise and was greeted by a very large frozen puddle. We were on the floor in seconds and while there was no damage I concluded that my green laning had to be done solo from then on which, in the short term, meant club runs. At least my timing was good. The first meeting of Pete's nascent club was held the following week and there was a good turn-out. There was a fair spread of ages, though I was easily the youngest, and a run was arranged for a few Sundays ahead. The rendezvous point was a garage in Chirk, owned by one of the members, and it was here that I realised age wasn't the only difference between us.

By the time a group of about ten bikes had gathered, mine was the only Japanese machine among them. The others were all big British singles or twins. The Yamaha looked out of place and, while I wasn't going to turn round and go home with my tail between my legs, I certainly felt self-conscious. As self-conscious as a rider who arrived on a Triumph twin, clearly more immaculate than the others. I pondered his chances as we set off in line astern, with the lead rider soon diving off the main road onto a small unassuming looking track. He certainly knew the area as we covered about eight short tracks in the next couple of hours, the paths varying from muddy lanes to rocky streams.

After completing each track, we rarely had to ride more than a couple of miles on tarmac before starting another and, despite my misgivings at the Yamaha sticking out so obviously, I really enjoyed the ride. My biggest concern before the start was whether I'd be able to keep up with these bigger, more powerful machines, but I needn't have worried. Maintaining the same pace was no trouble at all and on the muddier tracks the light weight of my Yamaha was a distinct advantage. It was obvious really, though perhaps hard for traditionalist to accept at the time. 500cc singles were still the preferred off-road mount, with the bigger-is-better mentality deeply entrenched. Though I shouldn't criticise, look at the monster off-roaders marketed today. They're totally unsuited to tough, muddy going, which the nervous Triumph rider that I had noticed at the start of the run was experiencing back on our club run in 1974. He was not having fun. This was obviously his first time and he tried to ride his Triumph as if he was on the road. He fell frequently, had to be helped through the mud and when we stopped for a break, his Triumph was overheating so badly he had to call it a day. *'Tough luck'* I thought, as otherwise the first club run had been a success; everyone agreed they were up for another.

The best news for me was my little Yamaha's performance. Its light weight and responsive engine helped no end, though one obvious shortcoming was that I had the wrong gearing. The DT needed a much lower bottom gear off-road, to cope with the tougher conditions. Most of the time on the lanes, I rarely got higher than second gear which indicated that I was hopelessly over-geared. To rectify this I ordered a larger rear sprocket from Roger Maughling, at Supersprox in Knighton, Mid-Wales, who was very helpful in dealing with my embarrassingly inept, novice questions. He advised on the number of teeth he thought would suit my needs and once the bigger rear sprocket was fitted, along with an extra link or two in the chain, the bike was transformed. 1st, 2nd and 3rd gears were all now useable on the lanes though as a downside, on the road, the top speed was considerably curtailed. I could still *cruise* at about 50mph, but that was now flat out in top. At the same time I fitted an engine decompressor in place of the blanking plug in the cylinder-head. This device, operated by a lever on the handlebars, gave the same effect as engine braking on a four-stroke and proved to be very useful on tricky descents. Things were rapidly getting very technical.

I thought I'd not see the Triumph rider again so was both pleased and surprised when he turned up at our next ride out. All had changed however. He'd evidently learnt as much as me on that last ride, probably more, as the Triumph was nowhere in sight. Instead he was on an Ossa Explorer, which was basically the Spanish manufacturer's full-on trials bike fitted with lights; a much more suitable machine and very much state-of-the-art. A number of riders also had the new Triumph TR5T Adventurer. This machine had a single-carburettor, 500cc Triumph twin engine in a BSA Victor frame and it certainly

The joys of off-roading. In this case man-handling an Ossa 310 through a bog at Ty Draw Farm, Bodfari, North Wales. This was a year later, in January, though my off-road *'skills'* were still rudimentary

looked the part. It was the best thing you could buy at the time if you wanted a larger off-road machine, and many did. The reason being – as I was finding out with my Yamaha - that the smaller trail bikes really weren't practical as day-to-day transport on the street. The Adventurer was practical both on and off road and as such the precursor to modern Adventure bikes. I was hugely envious, though I thought I'd still not be strong enough to manhandle such a bike, not least since, once we were out on the tracks, one Adventurer rider was really demonstrating how. He made everything look easy and seemed to float over the top of muddy bogs which all but swallowed the rest of us up. At a rest stop, I chatted with him, a quiet Liverpudlian. I was surprised by his ability, given his age - he must have been at least forty-five! – and when I complimented him, he just shrugged saying he'd been doing it a very long time. I had nothing like his ability, but as I gained experience, my confidence grew.

On a couple of occasions on that ride, I found myself immediately behind Pete Smith, who also rode a Triumph, and I could more or less match his pace. I smiled to myself as, while - from my Oulton Park experience – I knew road racing was never going to be my forte, this green laning was something that I thought I could crack. At another break, I chatted to the Ossa rider, a shipbuilder at Cammell Lairds. He also felt he was getting the hang of it and it was clear we were on the same page. Everything was falling into place, but the final piece of the jigsaw was sorting out riding alone. I solved that by persuading both my long-suffering - but, thankfully motorbike mad - girlfriend Steff and brother Dave to buy bikes similar to mine. Luckily, they agreed, so Steff's Yamaha 80 and Dave's Honda CB175 were part-exchanged for Yamaha DT125s identical to mine. In retrospect I should have asked Westminster Motorcycles for commission but that wasn't number one in my mind. My priority was company, and once Steff and Dave had run their bikes in, we made the same modifications that I had made to my own. Thankfully they both took to the lanes. They loved the experience, and it marked the start of a hectic and highly enjoyable period of about three years. Every weekend when I wasn't road testing a bike, regardless of the weather or season, the three of us would be out on the green lanes of North Wales. We really honed our skills over that period and I've certainly never been fitter in my life.

With the benefit of hindsight, off-road riding was also the best thing I could have done to improve my road riding. 1973/4 was pretty much the first time we saw American road racers in the UK and we marvelled at how a bunch of Californians could beat British road racers in the wet. During the Easter Transatlantic meetings, which were held at Brands Hatch, Mallory Park and my local Oulton Park, the likes of Kenny Roberts, Gene Romero and Dave Aldana dazzled us with their skills, honed on American dirt tracks. Now of course all the top road racers practice off-road, so I was simply ahead of my time!

Chapter 2
Team Observer

Road racing wasn't actually in my thoughts over the winter of 1974 but, out of the blue, road racing was about to throw my column a lifeline. Following my Norton and Laverda road tests I was at a bit of a loss as to how to fill my section of the paper. We ran a: *'Win a Revell Harley-Davidson Electra Glide kit'* competition, to run alongside the launch of the film Electra Glide in Blue at the local cinema, as well as a few other rather tangential pieces, such as rally reports and even clothing reviews, but they were stocking fillers really. I was clutching at straws and when I was summoned to the Managing Director's office I was worried. This was an extremely rare occurrence for anyone as lowly as me and, on my way, I racked my brain trying to think of what I might have done to incur the wrath of Mr G. Thomas. Was Motorcycle Scene for the chop?

I was actually warmly welcomed by Glyn, as he was *Glyn* when things were going well, though I put this down to him having a bit of a soft spot for me, as he had been a school friend of my uncle Paul who was killed in the war; but not so. He was evidently excited for another reason, and the instructions that he gave me in his oft-imitated - but never to his face - sing-song voice, came as a total surprise. I was to go to Oulton Park the next day, in order to meet someone who lived in his village. This person was going to be testing a sidecar outfit and, if he decided to buy it, the Cheshire Observer would be sponsoring him for the 1975 season. Glyn told me to get the full details, along with some photos, as these would constitute my next column.

I knew none of this was down to me, it was far too early for Motorcycle Scene to have had any impact, but it showed that my efforts were being viewed in a positive light, even if this development was pure luck. I stood up to leave and almost as an afterthought Glyn told me who the chap was that I needed to talk to: his name was Allen Steele. The next morning, I drove my company car into Oulton Park thinking, *I'm getting paid for this.'* It was busy, but I soon found Allen who had been

Allen Steele and Tony *'Adjers'* Barrow on the Cheshire Observer sponsored BSA A65. I couldn't have dreamt where our first cold meeting in 1975 would lead us

briefed by Glyn as to who I was and why I was there. From the off Allen proved to be a larger-than-life personality; a tough, strong character who didn't mince his words. I liked him immediately, especially as I discovered that he had a wicked sense of humour. I was only briefly introduced to his passenger Tony however, as they were quickly out on to the circuit, barely giving me a chance to have a look at the outfit we had come to see. A cursory glance told me that it was powered by a ubiquitous BSA A65 twin however, probably fitted with a Devimead 750cc top-end.

It certainly sounded well as the pair circulated, getting steadily faster as they put in some practice laps. To my inexperienced eye, it looked as if Allen and Tony had been doing this for ages. They were both fast and smooth and, when they returned to the pits, the owner of the outfit, Nev Riley, laughingly called to Allen, *'Where's your money then mate?'* Allen had set himself a target. When he was a solo racer his best lap on a 250 Yamaha around Oulton Park had been 80mph. He said that if he could match that speed, he'd buy the outfit. Allen and Tony had lapped at 81mph so that was it; with a quick handshake the deal was done.

As the details were being settled, I took the opportunity to take some pictures and get a bit of history from Allen. His name was new to me so he gave me the full run-down. He had been a successful solo rider in the 1960s but retired after winning the 1970 Lightweight Manx Grand Prix. He said at the time that he'd been physically and financially drained but now, as he was missing racing so much, he fancied coming back, but trying a new challenge. He was coming back, but trying an extra wheel. That probably sounds like madness today, giving up solos having won a Manx Grand Prix, to start on the bottom rung of sidecar racing. The thing is that sidecar racing was *huge* in the early 1970s. It was difficult to even get race entries and within a few years of Allen's entry into the sport both George O'Dell and Jock Taylor would emerge from the same scene as World Champions. Nigel Rollason did exactly the same thing as Allen too, winning the Manx Grand Prix on a solo the year after Allen then going on to race sidecars, very successfully: he won the Isle of Man TT. Participants and spectators alike *loved* sidecar racing. The switch wasn't as odd as it might seem today.

In Allen's case, to get going, he persuaded his brother-in-law, Tony Barrow - A.J. Barrow, known to one and all as *Adjers* - to passenger for him and then found out that Nev Riley was selling an outfit, Nev being a pretty decent National and TT runner. That's how he came to be at Oulton Park on that cold November morning and I kept in touch with Allen over the winter, visiting him on several occasions to see how things were coming along. On one such visit, Allen told me that he was having a pre-season practice at Oulton Park and as the outfit was now re-painted, he wondered if I would like to get some pictures. I went, and was pleased to see the outfit painted in yellow with the words *'Cheshire Observer'* in large black lettering down the side. It looked very professional, especially in the photograph they chose for the next issue of the paper. For Allen and Tony the session was a pre-season shakedown, to get to know the outfit better, and after they'd completed a few laps they stopped so we could chat. As we did so a couple of other guys in leathers turned up, obviously friends, jumped on the outfit and went out onto the circuit themselves. With everything that was going on, I didn't really pay attention, but remember thinking, *'Their helmets and leathers look familiar.'* As they pulled in Allen told me that they were TT stars John and Charlie Williams – unrelated - who, being friends of Allen, had come along for a bit of fun. The pair already had five TT wins between them and they'd go on to gain in total thirteen. John Williams would finish fifth in that year's 500cc World Championship and he'd beat Barry Sheene the following year, to win the Belgian Grand Prix.

What a gift. I had a *'scoop'* for the national motorcycle press. I had two genuine stars on a plate, except - typical of my luck and powers of observation - I had used up all my film. I still had a lot to learn and missing those photos wasn't my only cock-up as a rookie reporter that day. I made the classic mistake of not checking the correct, Celtic, spelling of Allen's name. I had him down as *Alan* in my column, but he didn't seem to mind. He was hugely pleased with the publicity I generated through the Observer and was even more delighted by the fact that I had sent a press release to the weekly motorcycling press. One of them, Motor Cycle, published it alongside a large copy of one of the photographs I had taken, which turned out to be a double positive. My Editor was also impressed, mainly to see a photo of the outfit bearing the words *'Cheshire Observer'* in a national publication. I hadn't done so badly after all.

The national coverage was great, but *National* wasn't where Allen was starting. Sidecars weren't solos and Allen's solo experience counted for little. He was starting on the bottom rung of the ladder again as three wheels were a completely different discipline to two. That meant racing at club level, joining several local racing clubs - in Allen's case these included the Wirral 100 Club and the Aintree Motorcycle Racing Club - and entering the events that they organised to gather points towards a new National racing licence.

Allen Steele in a previous life, before I knew him. Taking his second outing at the Manx Grand Prix, in 1966 on a Yamaha. He'd win the Lightweight Manx Grand Prix in 1970 on a similar 250cc machine

Despite Allen's considerable experience, he would also be required to wear a *'novice'* yellow jacket for the first part of the season. This was to indicate to other competitors Allen's presumed limited ability, but resulted in many experienced sidecar drivers being puzzled in due course by the sight of some no-name newcomer out-braking them into a corner which they thought that they had properly nailed. The first of these races was at Croft and, when I met Allen and Tony in the morning for the trip to the circuit in North Yorkshire, the outfit was already loaded into the race transporter. This sounds very grand but the transporter was in fact an old ambulance that became known to all and sundry as *The Jigger*. There wasn't a great deal of room in The Jigger with the outfit, leathers, helmets, tools and spares, so I had to scramble in the back and wedge myself into a corner. I wasn't complaining though. I'd watched races before, but now I was attending in a semi-official capacity, though that capacity wasn't precisely defined. Through association, I suppose I had some connection as a *representative of the sponsor*, but there again I was also unofficial photographer, PR man and dogsbody. I was potentially pusher too, as The Jigger wasn't blessed with much power and, fully loaded, the climb over the Pennines on the M62 was a struggle.

Irrespective, we managed to arrive at the circuit in plenty of time for scrutineering and practice. These went without a hitch, as did the first race, where Allen and Tony started well and proved to be competitive from the off. There were a number of outfits that were obviously faster on the straights, but Allen could hold his own through the corners and, while I know that I was already biased, the pair were clearly naturals on the bike. By the end of the meeting they'd taken several mid-field placings which was a superb showing for their very first event. As I would later discover testing on the road, just keeping all three-wheels in the same direction is challenging, racing an outfit is in a different league. The season ahead looked promising. Critically we had all enjoyed ourselves too, which in my case came from taking plenty of action pictures along with copious notes. These would make for a very different sort of column the following Friday and after subsequent meetings. But *different*, not necessarily *good*; photography in 1974 wasn't as it is today.

I already had an interest in photography and I wanted, wherever possible, to take my own. I also knew I'd have to. The Observer had a staff photographer, all local papers did, but he was often busy elsewhere when I needed photos taken locally and at some obscure race circuit, over a weekend, well, it was never going to happen. By chance and luck, the Assistant Advertising Manager Bob Edwards was a keen amateur photographer. As such he sold me a second-hand

Pentax SV SLR camera, along with a couple of lenses, as I'd need these and a camera of this type to produce print quality images. He also taught me the rudiments of operating the camera, which was the important bit, as there was no point-and-shoot back then. SLR - Single Lens Reflex – cameras were complex items, both in terms of their use and manufacture. They were rarities too, not least because of their price. Out of interest I looked at the price of the camera, new, and in 1965 when it was launched it was £110. That would be £2,325 in 2024 money, which shows you just why they were so thin on the ground.

Luckily I found quite early on that I could produce reasonable results, even on action shots, though it was always a case of fingers crossed. Today you see the quality of your photo the minute you take it. You can take another, hundreds if you want, until you get it right. Back then, I would take my pictures on film provided by the Observer, then give the roll of exposed film to Keith, the darkroom technician, to be processed. It was always black and white, twenty four or thirty six shots per roll, as colour gave much poorer quality and the Observer was all black and white images anyway. Keith would disappear into his darkroom and perform the dark arts of development, then give me a 'contact sheet' showing all the pictures the same size as on the film. That's to say tiny, 3cm by 2cm images or similar, from which I would choose a photograph for the column. Keith would then go back and print it full size, which was really the first time you could tell if you'd caught a good one or whether it was all fuzzy and blurred. My first attempt was at this initial Allen Steele meeting and, thankfully, it was a success. Glyn Thomas was very happy, both with the race results and my report, and especially with the pictures. Any image of the 'Cheshire Observer BSA' went down very well with him, so he encouraged me to keep attending and snapping away.

As it was, I didn't actually get to as many meetings as I would have liked. The fact was that Steff and I were soon to be married and all our spare time was taken up getting our new house habitable in time for our wedding. There was a solution to the reporting problem however. On the Monday following each meeting, I'd turn up at Allen's around dinner time, when he would give me a blow by blow account of that weekend's racing. Obviously, this wasn't as good as being there, but Allen told a good tale and I turned it into a column.

One meeting that I did manage to get to was a real historic curio. A recent change in the Road Traffic Act - April 2017 springs to mind - brought in legislation which removed the requirement for an expensive and time-consuming Act of Parliament to obtain a closed-road racing permit. i.e. a permit to allow racing on the UK's roads, as on the Isle of Man. It's not happened yet, but the truth is that it was taking place on Merseyside in the 1970s anyway. The New Brighton races were a unique annual event, which went on for decades, as the only event on the mainland where public roads were legally closed to allow motorcycle racing. The track went along the promenade, down King's Parade, west to east, and then back along Coastal Drive, negotiating several roundabouts - the wrong way - in the process. Well, in 1974 Allen and Tony went brilliantly, finishing in the top ten.

What I remember most about the meeting however was the informality on the event, both on and off the track. There were a couple of pretty St. John's Ambulance First Aid nurses stationed at one of the roundabouts and, on every lap and despite the fact that he was hanging off the *chair* at the time, Tony would give them a wave. Additionally, as I had a Press Access Pass, I was allowed trackside to take photos. In those days this really meant trackside, i.e. feet lodged firmly on the tarmac, though obviously off the racing line. I was happy snapping away but what really underlined the nature of those pre-Health & Safety days was what happened at the end of the race.

As the outfit approached me on the in lap, Allen slowed down and gestured for me to jump on. Without thinking, I did, Tony somehow making room on the platform for me to wriggle on. Allen then set off again and, while it may not have been full racing speed, it felt pretty rapid to me. I had no helmet of course, so it was a real white knuckle ride back to the paddock, during which I tried not to show that my hands were shaking. I knew there and then that sidecar passengering wasn't for me and if I hadn't, a subsequent visit to Aintree would have made up my mind for me; it was lined with railway sleepers!

The Observer BSA at New Brighton. These promenade racers were unique to the Merseyside seaside resort of Wallasey. Organised by the Wirral 100 Club they lasted into the 1990s until the dread hand of Health & Safety took its toll

Aintree was another Merseyside track, of about one and a half miles in length, using half of the old Formula One Circuit where Stirling Moss had won the 1955 British Grand Prix. It's still used today, located right next to the Grand National horse racing course. It features a very long straight, the Railway Straight and when Allen raced there, time and time again he would pass other outfits through the right-hand bend at Beechers, only to have faster machines, such as the Hillman Imp-engined outfit of Keith Galtress, power past him on the straights again. Even so, Allen and Tony managed a top ten finish and later in the season they did a lot better at Lincolnshire's Cadwell Park, one of the twistiest circuits in the UK.

I didn't manage to get to that meeting but the day afterwards there was a show at Chester Castle and Glyn Thomas had arranged for us to display the outfit. I didn't know how Allen and Tony had got along at Cadwell until I saw the two trophies. They were for a pair of third places, their best results of an excellent first season as despite not having the fastest outfit, they clocked up consistent mid-field finishes. Unfortunately, we already knew that there was no money to extend the Observer's sponsorship. While everyone I knew at the paper was fully in favour, other directors were rather more stuffy, establishment men, who didn't much care for oily motorcyclists. That didn't stop my own continued involvement however, particularly as Allen had already decided that there would be a new, more competitive outfit for the next season. He was committed and I'd become totally hooked.

Allen and Tony with some early trophies. I think these were from Cadwell Park, though my old negatives say, *'Possibly Darley Moor?'* It could be either, they did well at both

Chapter 3
Saved by the Germans

After the publication of the Norton and Laverda road tests, I had naïvely hoped I would be besieged by offers of test bikes from local dealers. It felt like a trickle but, looking back on my columns, I found that between May 1974 and February 1977, I actually tested thirty eight bikes of all shapes and sizes; not bad for a cub-reporter on a small provincial newspaper. It was a golden period for the industry, but I'd be hard pushed now to *name* thirty-eight different models made over that period; it's a lot. Those tests, written over forty years ago, make me cringe rather now as they weren't really tests at all, more like impressions. I didn't do any speed, acceleration or brake testing and, as much of the riding was done in my own time, I often wasn't able to cover huge mileages. I wasn't a good enough or sufficiently experienced rider at the time to really test a bike's capabilities to the limit either. The other obvious limitation of my reports was that I simply didn't have the column inches. MCN or BIKE magazine might cover five or six pages with a test but, reflecting back, did all those 0-60 figures, wheel-base measurements and turning circles really stack up to much?

I tried to provide a general feeling of what each bike was like to ride. I provided enough for buyers to know what they'd experience and perhaps this was equally as useful? I contented myself with the thought that, as riders weren't generally able to get test rides in those days, I was doing it for them, particularly as we might have the same levels of ability and skill. BIKE magazine would relish extolling a bike's wheelie-ing ability, but once you'd thrown your L-plates away who was really interested in that? For me, my rather more practical approach boiled down to nearly forty machines, which are far too many to regale you with here. Certainly some stood out however and after my initial Norton and Laverda tests it was bigger bikes which continued to roll in; '*Superbikes*' as they were becoming known in the 1970s. Had I been thinking logically, I would have drawn up a list of bikes that readers would have been most interested in and then tried to persuade dealers to let me borrow them. Instead, as a general rule, I was happy to receive whatever was offered. However, saying this, after the Laverda test, on a high and an impulse I took the, *'If you don't ask you don't get'* approach and, to my surprise, I scored a big hit, the first time I tried.

Riding the Laverda had given me a taste for the exotic and unusual and at that time nothing ticked those boxes like a BMW. Those big Bavarian bikes are some of the most common machines on the road today, but in the early 1970s they were rarely seen, partly as they were hugely expensive. They had until recently been considered the preserve of rich old gentlemen and were not for ordinary riders, the likes of you and me. Rock musicians Cozy Powell and I think Keith Emerson were photographed on them, but so too were the comedian Dick Emery and the actor Sir Ralph Richardson, neither of whom did much to boost the bikes' youth appeal. BMW's virtues were reliability and dependability; characteristics which, while laudable, were anything but cool. However, the introduction of the /5 series models saw massive investment by BMW at their Spandau factory, to where motorcycle production had switched in 1969. It saw the start of a wholesale modernisation programme for their range of flat twins, which by the early 1970s benefitted from new telescopic front forks and a big weight reduction over previous models.

By the time I was looking at getting my hands on one the bikes had received further updates, on the release of the /6 model series, which went hand in hand with a clever marketing campaign. It was designed to convince British riders that even though they were expensive, the Teutonic marvels were worth every penny. The introduction of front disc brakes on all but the smallest iteration, the R60/6, brought the machines even more up to date and sales were slowly increasing. Getting my hands on one of these updated BMWs was my objective but I thought I'd hit a brick wall before I'd even started. My research revealed what I should have known already: there were no BMW dealers locally, none even close. Rather than giving up without a fight and thinking, *'What have I got to lose?'* I took a deep breath, found BMW's phone number and called the importers in Chiswick. Trying to sound as professional as possible, explaining to the receptionist who I was, but probably fluffing it, I was put through to the Public Relations Manager,

Jeremy Fraser, who politely listened to my request, asked for a few more details and then said, *'No problem! Which bike would you like first?'* First! I was totally taken aback and as a result probably came out with the most unprofessional response imaginable. Instead of demonstrating my comprehensive and in-depth knowledge of every model and variation in their range I simply said, *'Oh, I'd be happy with anything.'* It was like that first day in Tom Loughridge's shop all over again, as the Public Relations man's telephone line went silent. Thankfully he was just checking on availability, as suddenly, out of the silence came, *'I can let you have an R75/6 for about a week if you like?'* Adding, *'I can bring it up to Chester for you, on a trailer, and collect it at the end of the test.'*

I had been expecting to get no more than a flea in my ear, a blank refusal. But true to his word, Jeremy arrived as arranged a week later and seemed genuinely excited that a local, regional, weekly newspaper had a motorcycling column. Perhaps my earlier claim that the Observer would be the first in the country was no idle boast, though realistically the lack of a BMW outlet probably swung it. BMW would have wanted one in the North West so having their bikes in the biggest local newspaper might have piqued the interest of a major dealer. Whichever way, he promised to loan me the full range of test bikes at his disposal and, before heading off back down south, he showed me over the R75. I had a long, hard look at it before setting off to ride it home, as everything about the machine exuded quality; I could see why they were such an expensive beast. I had never ridden a flat twin before and I had heard all of the old wives' tales about the rocking motion of the engine upsetting the handling. Back then ninety-nine percent of such stories came from people who'd never seen a BMW, let alone ridden one, but I wasn't reassured when I pressed the starter button, heard a strange mechanical noise as the starter gear engaged and felt the bike lean first to one side and then the other. *'Here goes nothing'* I thought as I put it into first gear, which engaged with that audible clunk well known to generations of BMW riders. I wondered if I would be able to get used to the bike's idiosyncrasies, though Jeremy Fraser's parting words rung in my ears, *'BMWs take a bit of getting used to, but stick with it, they're worth it.'*

I heeded his words as I negotiated the rush hour traffic, the bike feeling so different to anything I'd ever ridden before. That was probably due to those huge protruding cylinders, one either side, neither quite in line with the other and I still wasn't sure if I would ever adapt to it. I'll admit that to start with I found it to be rather strange. I was used to filtering through the traffic on my slim little DT125, but there was no chance of that on the BMW. However, after a longer ride into North Wales the next day I began to get to grips with the R75. The further I travelled on the BMW the more I relaxed. It was smooth, quiet, powerful in an understated sort of way - in those days, 50bhp was quite an acceptable figure - and undeniably very comfortable. I could understand why BMWs were the machine of choice for so many long distance touring riders. It was both easier and more relaxing to ride than either the Norton or Laverda and clearly something that would have been very easy to live with. This was in complete contrast to what I tested next.

BMWs are a common sight today, but in the mid-1970s the flat-twins were viewed as incredibly exotic, luxury machines and not for the likes of you or me. There was not much to choose between any of the models, they were all fabulous

Despite my best efforts in trying to secure road test bikes from local dealers, I still felt I was struggling. I know this might sound rather arrogant, but I thought that off the back of three Superbike tests and my wonderful prose, I would have been inundated with spontaneous offers. Of course, nothing of the sort had happened, but I wasn't to know that it could be much the same for the glossy monthlies. They weren't flooded with offers either, even if this is what one might have assumed. I realised I'd have to cast my net further and, after I showed Birkenhead dealer, Mike Weston of Mike Weston Motorcycles a copy of my Laverda test, he offered me his Ducati GT750 demonstrator. That by anyone's standards was a result. Ducati twins were even rarer on the roads than BMWs. This was a shower of riches.

When I first set eyes on the orange and black V-twin - often known as an 'L' twin - it was awe inspiring. It was long, lean and low and I couldn't wait to ride it. Also, I was intrigued to experience a bike with an engine configuration that I hadn't come across before. I'd heard that V-twins were smooth and produced plenty of torque, so I was eager to find out if this was the full story. The bike and I didn't get off to a good start however as the kick-start was positioned in such a way that a long swing ensured that your shin engaged the footrest, with full force, some time before your foot completed the full radius of its arc. Ouch! I wore the scars for quite a while and so did many other owners. Compared to the BMW the Ducati kick-start/footrest arrangement was an ergonomic disaster. You wondered how such an arrangement could have passed testing, but incredibly many Italian bikes continued with these quirks. Clip-on handlebars matched with forward set footrests and unmarked switch gear which was impossible to use with a gloved hand were typical. You were expected to accept these as *'character'* on *'enthusiasts'* machines and I discovered more of the Ducati's character while pulling away. It wasn't at all smooth. It was horribly lumpy actually, but this was mainly as it didn't want to run on both cylinders. I didn't think much of the dealer's machine preparation but I persevered and after a couple of miles the 375cc single transformed into 750cc. The other spark plug cleared itself and I was suddenly on a beautiful sounding, rasping, V-twin. I was probably hasty to blame the dealer. It was a case of, *'Sorry sir, they all do that.'*

Once properly underway, the Ducati in fact felt very similar to the Laverda as it had a similarly long wheelbase. However at 407lbs it was a massive 100lbs lighter than the other Italian twin and carried its weight lower too. As a consequence it was easier to throw around, with the bevel-drive V-twin engine an absolute delight. The amount of torque available at any throttle opening was awesome, with the throttle cables seemingly connected directly to the back wheel. As I only had the bike for a weekend, Steff and I agreed to ride up to Ambleside to visit a friend of ours who worked there at the time. The Ducati coped with this ride in an effortless fashion, loping along in top gear on just a whiff of throttle, yet at a consistently high speed. Unlike the 750 BMW it was a bike that needed a high level of concentration to get the best out of it, but the effort was richly rewarded. I wasn't really sure how practical the GT750 would be as an everyday bike – that kick-start alone would be enough to put you off - but riding it was a special experience, which could equally be said of my next test machine.

Out of the blue, soon after, I got another phone call from Jeremy Fraser, *'I've got an R90S on a trailer here for you, I can bring it up and you can have that for a week too.'* I couldn't wait. This was BMWs top-of-the-range model and come the day I was presented with a beautiful, smoke grey and silver example. They only came in two colour schemes, Smoke Grey and Daytona Orange, the latter of which faded a bright orange into a lighter shade which was almost silver. Both were stunning and set a new standard in paintwork. Classy, but also very 1970s, in a metal-flake, in your face, sort of way. With its cockpit fairing, twin drilled front disc brakes and huge Dell'Orto carburettors, it could be nothing less than the flagship of their fleet, though also a monument to incremental development. Under the skin it wasn't vastly different to the drum-braked 600cc model, demonstrating what a big impact just a few tweaks and updates could make.

These tweaks weren't just skin deep however, the engine was heavily breathed on. After my time with the R75/6, I was familiar with the feel of a BMW flat-twin, but I wasn't prepared for the urgency of the R90's engine. I knew that it had a high-compression motor, developing 67bhp care of the accelerator pump-equipped carburettors, and these

Free Press Day show tickets were one perk of the job, even if you had to lean over the professional photgraphers' shoulders. The models were for them, not for us

contributed to much enhanced get-up-and-go. It went much better than I'd hoped however and I felt that such a special bike deserved a special test. Luckily one dropped into my lap. The following weekend the North Wales Green Lane Riders had organised a few days' trail riding in the Brecon Beacons, in South Wales. Steff and I had neither a trailer for our Yamahas, nor money for hotels, so we had reluctantly declined the invitation on the grounds of our pre-nuptial poverty. Now, we would ride down on the Sunday morning, in time to have breakfast with them, and then turn around and ride home again. This three hundred mile round trip would be a good chance to find out what the R90S was all about.

Come the day I picked Steff up from her parent's house before the sun was up and pointed the BMW south, out of Chester towards Wrexham. It was then through Newtown and Builth Wells and on to Brecon. Once away from the built-up areas, I picked up speed, the power of the *'Boxer'* motor and the wind protection from the surprisingly effective cockpit fairing making a high average speed child's play. The R90S was pretty much the first motorcycle ever to come equipped with a fairing as standard and riding it made me wonder why no other manufacturer did the same. They eventually would, but behind the fairing I really got into a groove and covered the ground very quickly. Remember, this was early on a Sunday morning, the weather was good and speed cameras hadn't been invented.

As we clocked up the miles, I reflected that this was a machine that could flatter even an average rider. I couldn't get anywhere near the limits of the machine's handling and I loved the novelty of the singing sound made by the perforated twin discs when braking from high speed; it just added to a totally involving riding experience. We were at the hotel before 8:30, in time for a good chat with our friends over breakfast and, while I expected to be envious that they were preparing for a day's green lane riding, I actually couldn't wait to get back on the BMW again. The ride back was just as good, with us arriving one and a half hours earlier than we'd expected, both fresh due to the supreme levels of comfort. Niggles? Well, the tall carburettors dug into my shins a bit, but that was it. The R90S was a sublime motorcycle on which you could ride in matchless comfort. This was not something I experienced on my next BMW test ride, but Bavaria couldn't be blamed for that.

At a stroke the R90S had made BMWs interesting to ordinary motorcyclists and the whole range was now attracting a lot of scrutiny. In the spring I was offered the other R90, the R90/6, and as this was a less focussed machine than its stable-mate it was obviously very appealing. There was only one catch; on this occasion I would have to go down to Chiswick to collect it. There was no way I was going to turn down the offer however, so I went down by train the Thursday before the Easter Bank Holiday weekend, to be picked up by Jeremy at the station. It was hardly fun navigating the Great West Road and then the North Circular in heavy, pre-holiday, traffic on someone else's expensive motorbike, but eventually I was on the M1 heading north, where the R90/6 really came into its own. The thing was as I rode on, the skies were becoming ominously dark and I was getting colder and colder. Before I had ridden more than twenty miles, it began to snow and in no time at all the tarmac disappeared. The motorway became white and the traffic was reduced to a crawl. Those of a certain vintage will remember 1976 as the super-hot year of the drought. Less well remembered is the snow of the Easter the year previously. Climate change? Tell me about it!

From around Birmingham onwards, I was forced to ride in second gear, with the engine just off tick-over, both feet hanging down. I was constantly pelted by snow and slush thrown up by vehicles passing moderately faster and I soon lost all feeling in my hands and toes. I was dressed 1970s-style, for spring, I wasn't prepared for this. I also had only enough cash for fuel and a cup of tea or two, which was obviously a big mistake given that credit cards were still for film stars and VIPs. I was soon on the verge of hypothermia, but luckily I decided to do the only thing that I could: I pressed on. I counted the miles down to every single motorway service area, where in time-honoured fashion I would warm my hands and then my gloves under the hand driers in the toilets. I even directed the warm air nozzle into my over-trousers to try to get warmer, which got me some suspicious looks. At each stop, through rationing, I scraped together just enough spare cash to buy a cup of tea and I savoured it before gritting my teeth and setting off again.

I was dreading conditions on the 'A' roads when I left the M6 in Cheshire, as I'd have to negotiate bends, junctions and roundabouts, but I needn't have worried. Not long after I left the motorway, the snow stopped and the roads were magically clear. After two hundred miles and eight and a half hours, I arrived home, but being unable to get off the bike, I sounded the horn repeatedly until my dad came out to see what all the fuss was about. As soon as he saw the layers of ice on my headlamp and knees, he understood and came out to help me off. My family had been worried, as had Jeremy Fraser. He had phoned hours before, to enquire if I had arrived, and my dad had promised that I would ring him as soon as I got in. I did, but only after downing a big mug of tea, heavily laced with whisky. Jeremy was relieved to receive my call as he told me that within half an hour of my departure conditions in London had become horrendous. Things were so bad that the famous Transatlantic motorcycle races at Brands Hatch, which were due to take place the next day, Good Friday, were cancelled. As a footnote, Sunday's round of the race incredibly took place in the snow at Mallory Park, while on Monday, at local Oulton Park, all was miraculously clear.

For me thawing out in a hot bath was both agony and ecstasy, but as I lay there trying to get some feeling back into my body, I reflected on what a wonderful motorbike that 900cc BMW really was. Not only had it not missed a beat, but when the chips were down, in such extreme conditions, it had needed minimal input from me. To this day, I'm convinced that no other bike would have got me home safely and to prove my trust, the next day, after a good night's sleep and a thaw, it was a pleasure to ride the R90/6 under normal road conditions. The best thing about the 60bhp engine was that there was no discernible power-band; the bike quite literally pulled from nothing, making it very easy to ride. Of course, after such an experience, I wrote a glowing report and with hindsight and fifty years' additional experience my assessment would still be exactly the same.

My favourite middleweight. The R60/6 which I only got to test later on. Though the smallest BMW it was beautifully balanced and refined

Chapter 4
Riding a TT Winner

Despite riding other people's bikes and – sort of - getting paid for it, I was still green laning at the weekends, now with Steff and Dave. At the time Llyn Brenig was being constructed, a new reservoir on the Denbigh Moors and there were miles of unmade, accessible, construction tracks. These were deserted at the weekend and we enjoyed them to the full, often with other TRF riders. The North Wales Green Road Riders' Club was also still thriving, but we weren't riding on as many of their runs as they were travelling further afield, often taking their bikes on trailers and stopping overnight. For a young couple setting up home and about to get married this was sadly out of the question, though we managed a couple of runs.

One was in Derbyshire, where I was able to borrow a VW van from work, to take both my bike and David's. We rode many little lanes that day, largely between dry stone walls, covering a good few miles though through lack of familiarity I have no idea where. The other run, we rode high into Snowdonia in the depths of winter. On one of the days, riding through Betws-y-Coed, we suddenly turned left up an insignificant track by the Shell garage which was, apparently, an ancient Roman Road; the steepest one that I had ever seen. It was a severe climb up a rocky track, which really tested both me and my machine. I was extremely pleased to have made the summit unaided as other riders weren't so lucky, many really struggled.

Later on that run, high in the mountains, we were on a fast flat section when I was passed by a bike that seemed to float over all obstacles. When we stopped, I saw that it was a Swedish Monark 125. A tiny thing really, from a marque now largely forgotten. The small, bespectacled Welshman who rode it had apparently won a Gold Medal in the International Six Days Trial and it didn't surprise me at all. It was no wonder I couldn't live with him. It wasn't all competitive however; we had some fun. Stan Whittaker was a great bloke who loved the club runs. He owned an immaculate red MZ ISDT Replica, which everyone admired. People think of MZs as cheap commuters but these bikes were very special; hand-built and very fast. Stan turned up for this particular run in a brand-new TT Leathers fabric suit which was red to match his bike. He looked like a model out of one of those 1970s Lewis Leathers adverts, so we conspired to arrange our bikes in such a way that when we set off we covered him in mud. To be last in line wasn't his choice, but his language certainly was!

Perhaps I shouldn't have laughed, as not long after, Steff, David and I went back, to ride some of the tracks again. We knew them a bit better now and on a fast, flat-out bit, riding quite quickly, I felt a bang on my left foot, followed by a sharp, stabbing pain. It would teach me to ride with my feet sticking out, as I'd caught my foot on a big rock when I wasn't totally on the ball. The pain really was pretty bad and I knew that if I took my boot off I'd probably not get it back on; but it was also so painful that I wouldn't be able to change gear as it was. We were about sixty miles from home; what could I do? After pondering for a few minutes, the tools came out and I moved the gear lever upwards through 90°. Now, with a little effort, I could reach down and change gear by hand. It was awkward, but it got me home. Once rested, there was no long-term damage, which was more than could be said for my now long-suffering DT125. Not long after, riding back from North Wales, the Yamaha suddenly slowed. I thought that it had just fluffed a spark plug, so I took the plug out to find some extra metal attached to the central electrode. Fearing the worst, I tentatively stuck a screwdriver down the plug hole and found thin air where there shouldn't have been any - in the piston crown! The poor thing had put up with being thrashed without mercy for years – it was only a 125cc after all – and had finally cried, *'Enough!'*

Despite the pressures, both on time and money, the Yamaha was treated to a rebore and I even managed to get to the TT. It was only for a day, but my brother and I did what many did at the time, which was to take the midnight boat from Liverpool, catching the reverse crossing back again. By 1975 the programme had been re-hashed, moving the Senior race from its traditional, prime-time Friday slot, to make way for what was now seen as the Blue Riband event, the Classic

Stan Whitaker with his immaculate ISDT Replica MZ and equally immaculate riding gear, shortly before getting covered in mud

race. The Senior was now on the Wednesday, so we were looking forward to seeing this, along with the 500cc Sidecars. We were early, at a good spot, but standing at Governor's Bridge I was aware that people close by were nudging each other and surreptitiously pointing in our direction, so I turned to have a look. There was Mike Hailwood, standing like the rest of us punters, waiting to see what passed us by, which in this case were largely two-strokes.

Over the years they'd nibbled away at the smaller classes but it was interesting to see how they were now dominating the 500cc class too, as was demonstrated in the race, where Chas Mortimer initially led. He was on a '352cc' Yamaha – almost inevitably a *Fablon Special*', a 350cc simply carrying 500cc plates – and was fast until slowed by a lengthy pit stop. This allowed Heswall rider John Williams - also on a '352cc' Yamaha - to lead until lap five, when Mick Grant started to fly on his – genuine – 500cc Kawasaki triple. The finishing order was: Mick Grant, John Williams and Chas Mortimer, as the days of British singles on the rostrum were sadly over. Dave Hughes in thirteenth place was on the first four-stroke home. I managed to take some

Mike Hailwood riding pillion to Geof Duke on a Gold Wing. Later I'd be standing next to him at Governor's Bridge, where he was watching like all the regular punters

photographs however, including of all the local crew and they couldn't have been that bad. I gave Charlie Williams one and it eventually appeared, years later, when he got round to writing his own book. The other race that day was for the 500cc Sidecars where it was much the same story. The previous BMW stranglehold on the class was well and truly broken by the two-strokes. Top honours still went to a German crew, Rolf Steinhausen and Josef Huber, but they were on a Konig, a two-stroke engine originally designed for a speedboat. It was a sign of the times, but personally I was sad to see the BMWs ousted from top spot. As a footnote, there had been an epic, ten-lap, two-rider Production TT earlier in the week. I'd been disappointed to miss this as it featured several locally sponsored machines. I would like to have seen them, but as I was to find out, the opportunity hadn't entirely passed.

Steff and I were married in July, but a couple of weeks beforehand I got a phone call from Tom Loughridge. He asked if I could go to see him, as he had a proposition to put to me. His dealership had been awarded the coveted *'SuzukiServ'* status, due to the quality of his workmanship and facilities, and knowing what Tom had invested I wasn't surprised, but what had it got to do with me? *'I want to have a big promotional feature in the Observer, to advertise the award, and can arrange for a full-page advert, paid for by myself and my suppliers in the trade.'* He also asked if I could write an editorial, but there was an additional request too: *'Could you run a competition for readers?'* He had booked a lengthy session at Oulton Park and his idea was to run a fuel consumption test. He would put exactly one gallon of fuel in the tank of a Suzuki T500 and get me to ride around the circuit until the tank ran dry, *'Readers can then write in with their estimates of how far the bike will travel and I can provide a good prize.'* I was more than happy with the plan, as I knew my bosses would be too, but there was more to come. After the fuel consumption test, on the standard road going T500, Tom wanted me to ride his TT racing version. The very same bike that, with co-rider Ian Richards, Tom had led that year's 500 Production TT, until slowed by a faulty condenser. What an offer. I'd be paid to ride a TT bike, having bagged a huge advertising order.

As the road bike was available I planned to test that too, so I picked it up a few days later and actually rode it to our new house, on the morning of our wedding. At the time, Suzuki had all their eggs in the two-stroke basket and they were producing a good range of machines that sold well. This was not least because of their association with Barry Sheene, who started out with the company on a TR500, the water-cooled, racing version of the standard air-cooled road bike I was on. The T500's engine in comparison to Sheene's was obviously quite conventional and relatively unsophisticated. However, the 47hp that it produced gave the stroker a reasonable turn of speed and a lot more mid-range power than I had expected it to have. It was the first big two-stroke I'd ridden and that aspect really surprised me.

It wasn't peaky at all, quite the opposite. The bike wasn't heavy either and it handled reasonably well, so it was going to be easy to produce a good write-up. The only aspect letting the bike down being an unexpected one as there was a fair deal of vibration through the handlebars and footrests, something which I thought was confined to old British machines. As the final part of the test, and just four days after our wedding - and technically on the honeymoon which we never had - Steff and I found ourselves at Oulton Park, where once again brother David supplied the leathers and full-face helmet. I genuinely didn't have the cash to buy either myself.

As I was to be riding all day Bob Edwards came along to take the photographs, which began with one of the Suzuki's fuel tank being drained and exactly one gallon of petrol added back in. I then trundled around the track, waiting for the fuel to run out. This ride was enjoyable as I already knew the bike and, since the Norton test, I had some idea of where the track went. As I became more familiar with the circuit, I was able to ride progressively faster, though obviously not actually *fast*. I could hardly cane the thing, I was meant to be proving the machine's fuel-sipping credentials. As a result I actually completed quite a few laps, with the Suzuki averaging about 50mpg before spluttering to a halt.

It was the racer next and as this was a Production racer, it was ostensibly the same machine. I expected the transition to be easy, but there was one problem right from the start: the gears. The road bike had the traditional Japanese system; the gear lever on the left, with the down-for-first-gear, up-for-all-the-rest, pattern. The racer however had the gear lever on the right, with up for first gear and down for all the rest. This was because Tom, like most racers at the time, had cut his teeth on British bikes and had got used to the traditional pattern; it actually predominated for many years on race bikes. Though I'd had a Triumph 500 I was out of practice, and the change pattern was actually the reverse anyway. As such I rode carefully for the first few laps, concentrating on getting my footwork right. This was to the exclusion of all other considerations, which included the riding position, as the racer was far more focussed than the road bike.

I've never felt comfortable in a racing crouch, but it's horses for courses and I soon got the hang of it, even if the engine characteristics proved trickier. The racer had a narrower power band than the

Steff on the Suzuki T500 before we departed for Oulton Park. The track test constituted our honeymoon, as we'd only been married a few days and we never actually had one

roadster and was both smoother and much faster. Tom hadn't changed its overall gearing from when he'd ridden it at the TT either, where the bike had been clocked at 133mph through the speed trap at The Highlander. This made it the fastest Production 500 for some years and rather laid bare the claim that these were standard machines. Tom's was no different from any of the others however, they were all breathed upon and, for stability and better ground clearance at the TT, Tom had fitted nineteen inch wheels, front and rear.

It was all legal, as you could alter anything if it was from a safety point on view – raise pipes, foot-rests, etc – but this also took me a while to get used to. It was definitely sure-footed however, which was attested to by a little bit of history I didn't actually know. Before being Tom's, this very bike had won the 1970 500 Production TT, ridden by Frank Whiteway. I'd wondered about the Crooks Suzuki stickers on the bike, the explanation being that these were Frank's sponsors and the providers of the bike.

I was riding a bit of TT history without knowing it, and lapping steadily, gaining in confidence and building up speed when suddenly I got the fright of my life. As I approached Cascades, the downhill left-hander, at what I thought was a respectable speed, there was an almighty yowl as a works Suzuki came past me as if I was standing still. I recognised the helmet of another Cheshire rider, Stan Woods, and remembered that Tom had said that Stan would be doing a few laps to *run-in* a new engine. Any pretensions I had that I was lapping at a decent velocity were well and truly shattered: running in indeed! Having got back into the groove, I accelerated hard over Hilltop towards Knickerbrook and was actually travelling quite quickly in top gear. Perhaps I was over doing it in Stan's wake, trying to emulate him, as it was then that I noticed a small problem; a squirrel was sitting in the middle of the track, right on my intended line. Before I had time to do anything more than panic, the little creature calmly scampered off, but the thrills weren't quite over yet.

My colleague at the Observer, Bob Edwards, took this photo of me on the Tom Loughridge Production racer. In 1975 Tom and partner Ian Richards would have won the 10-lap Production TT on the same bike had a condenser wire not come adrift

Perhaps I was rattled, as on the next lap, accelerating hard out of Lodge, down into Deer Leap, I only went and changed down instead of up. I got my up-for-up, and down-for-down, mixed up and, not realising my error, I let the clutch out, in a lower rather than higher gear. The rear wheel locked, rubber screamed in protest, and the bike started to slew sideways. Luckily, I was on auto-pilot and without thinking I instantly whipped the clutch in again. What was clearly a very well-behaved bike straightened itself out without any further input from me. As is often the case in such eventualities, everything seemed to happen in slow motion and it sorted itself out all on its own. However, I distinctly remember coming over the crest onto the start/finish straight and seeing people running along the track side towards me. They were frit but I was frit too. I had to stay out for a couple more laps, to regain my composure, as I was shaking so much. Coming into the pits I thought how smug I'd been feeling previously, thinking I'd mastered the different shift patterns; pride cometh before a fall, though thankfully I'd avoided the falling.

There were no tears or broken motorcycles and my two tests – road bike and racer – went into the paper alongside my editorial piece on the SuzukiServ award. They were accompanied by some nice photos, with the addition of the advertisements from Tom Loughridge, Suzuki themselves – quite a coup - and a few of Tom's suppliers. It was more than a full page in total and when I took copies of the paper to Tom's shop he was over the moon.

There were two bigger outcomes however. My boss, Eric, was very happy with the money that the feature had brought in and from then onwards he actively encouraged me to devote more time to the column. Secondly, an unforeseen consequence of Tom's big feature was that other dealers couldn't fail to see it. To a man, it must have annoyed them that Tom Loughridge, a Midlander and upstart newcomer on the scene, was getting more publicity than them. Slowly but surely, dealers such as Bill Smith of Bill Smith Motors, Geoff Morgan at Davies Brothers and Alan Dugdale from Hector Dugdale Motors started to approach me with offers of road test models. The boot was on the other foot. It had taken me a while, but it looked like I was finally *in*.

I'd tested a few machines already, prestige ones at that, but, given that it was the 1970s, there was one obvious major engine configuration that had eluded me: the engine type that was, thanks to the Japanese, changing the whole face of motorcycling. I'm talking of course about the across-the-frame, four-cylinder, four-stroke engine, the UJM – Universal Japanese Motorcycle - first seen in the form of Honda's revolutionary and seminal CB750.

Although the CB750 was announced in 1969, we didn't see many here in the UK until the tail end of 1970. Having a hot line to the Honda management in Japan – he came very close to becoming the official importer - Chester dealer Bill Smith demonstrated the sensational new model around the Mountain Course at the 1970 TT and, luckily for me, the very same machine was on display before and after the meeting. It was in Bill's showroom, just a few minutes' walk from my house, so I was able to get a good look at it, when others weren't standing in my way; you can understand, it generated a lot of interest.

To my inexperienced eye, the Honda looked amazing, with a level of refinement that was hard to imagine. For the time the specification was almost beyond belief: electric start, disc brakes, overhead-camshaft, four cylinders, four silencers, five gears, 67 horsepower and a price of £649. Those were quite some stats, but the 750 also looked a big unwieldy thing; it would simply have been too much for me. It wasn't on my radar, but even back then I wondered if Honda might bring out a scaled-down, 500cc version......... and they must have been listening. I only had to wait until 1971 to hear about it and the paper specifications looked impressive; the bike had many of the features of its big brother but, importantly, it was 80lbs lighter, while still managing to better 100mph from its stated 50bhp. As I said, this was all on paper, I didn't get to ride one. Dealers didn't have demonstrators, they didn't need to. They could sell all they could get, which wasn't many. How was I going to get my hands on one? Well, by 1975, although Honda were still the only manufacturer producing a middleweight multi, they were more numerous and Tom Loughridge came to the rescue again.

The machine he had in stock was a real beauty and I was especially impressed by its two-tone colour scheme and four silencers which looked fantastic from the rear. Although fast enough for most riders, I found the 500-four a real pussy cat, being easy to ride and very civilised. The smoothness of the four-cylinder engine, even when high revs were used, amazed me, but those high revs did need to be used. The mid-range torque, compared to the big twins that I'd ridden recently, was minimal and a disappointment in many ways. The engine was quite tractable at low revs, but it didn't really *go* anywhere. To make progress it wanted lots of revs so thankfully the gear-change was positive; as tap-dancing was necessary to keep the engine on the boil. Also, while it sounds harsh to say it now, riding the Honda made me realise quite how well the Norton and Laverda handled: that was simply the truth. The Honda wasn't a bad handling machine, it just wasn't in the same league as the others. I didn't push it hard enough to

Bob Edwards at the controls this time, while I manned the Pentax. I often lacked photos of myself riding, simply as I had to test alone

really test its limits, but even at relatively sedate speeds the suspension and chassis showed that the Japanese still had a lot of catching up to do. The Honda was undeniably efficient and was to prove reliable but, for me at least, it wasn't very *involving*. That was the best word I could come up with at the time and it was a trait that I was to find with other four-cylinder machines over the years. Whilst they were objectively great bits of engineering, subjectively their character simply didn't do it for me. Perhaps I had been spoilt too early, by my experience with the lazy power of vertical, V, and horizontally-opposed big twins?

I got to test a few middleweights around this time, with the next being a real contrast to the Honda: Suzuki's mid-range three-cylinder two-stroke, the GT550. Behind the scenes Suzuki were working on the ground-breaking GS750 four-cylinder model, but, until it was launched in 1976, Suzuki still had an entirely two-stroke range. Above their learner-legal, sub-250cc bikes, the T500 was their only twin, as the rest were triples: the GT380, GT550 and the water-cooled GT750 and any would have been a first for me. I had never ridden a three-cylinder bike before though, like the 500 Honda, the GT wasn't quite what I'd expected. For a start the GT550 was no wheelie-ing, fire-breathing beast, like the superficially similar Kawasaki 500 triple.

The Suzuki was a very easy machine to get on with and the smoothest, quietest bike that I had ever tested. At 441lbs, it was formidably heavy for its size, but the bike had always been designed as a Grand Tourer, hence the 'GT' designation: it was deliberately over engineered. The engine was unstressed and would pull easily in any gear from below 3,500rpm. This helped its exemplary town manners, which were put to the test in its first public engagement as I was volunteered by the management at the Observer to lead the Mayor of Chester's annual parade. There I was on an unfamiliar bike, in front of a cheering crowd, complete with a supporting cast of brass bands and marching Scouts, ahead of the column through the city centre on a busy Saturday afternoon. Thankfully, apart from me feeling hideously self-conscious, it all went remarkably well. At walking pace there was a good deal of clutch slipping – the GT was meant for fast A-road cruising, it didn't have a particularly low first gear - but the bike kept its cool and coped admirably. Reading my test report back now the Bridgestone tyres were the only thing which came in for criticism; I actually said that I would throw them away. I can't possibly imagine that the tyres were really that bad, so I was probably just copying the *'proper'* motorcycle journalists' line at the time: rubbishing perfectly adequate Japanese rubber.

As such my one real criticism, which would stand the test of time, was fuel consumption of an alarming 35mpg. That would have been enough to drop it from my shopping list, though it was the oil crisis of the mid-1970s which really sounded the death knell for heavy drinkers of this type. Four-strokes were soon more popular again. It was timely then that it was back to Honda next, for a chalk-and-cheese, back-to-back test which summed up the diversity which was available in the mid-1970s, even from the same manufacturer.

Based on the revolutionary CB450 *'Black Bomber'*, which was Honda's first big bike, the CB500T twin should have been a good seller. They'd had nearly a decade to get it right, but didn't, as among other things Honda's styling department got this one seriously wrong. The looks of the bike were unusual but, worse still, was the horrible colour: brown. I know this shouldn't be the prime consideration, but most motorcyclists buy partly with their eyes, and this bike had looks which only a mother could love. The four-cylinder Honda CB500 and CB550 also came in brown and even the Moto Morini 250 and 350 could be bought in the same colour. But they got away with it somehow, while the Honda twin did not. The Honda even had a brown seat and, while that might be seriously fashionable among hipsters, it looked simply awful back in my day. In its defence the CB500T did most things competently, but it was soulless and exceptionally dull. Given all the excellent bikes around in the 1970s, who would ever buy one? Worse still, how could I recommend one?

I've covered this previously, but working for a local newspaper that relied on advertising for its survival, how could I denigrate a bike supplied by a dealer who was paying? Conversely, it was very hard for me to draw out any positives given something so exceptionally bland. Praise where I laid it was faint indeed and I left enough un-said so people could easily read between the lines. I don't think many would have rushed out and bought a CB500T as a consequence of reading my test, so that's how I squared it with my conscience. Oddly, since then, I've met riders who have owned and loved their 500Ts and I must have got the balance right in my write-up as the dealer certainly didn't complain. Far from it, I was actually offered another Honda. This was cut from an entirely different cloth and you have to cast your mind back here, to exactly how big this particular bike was built up to be. There had been a 350-four, a couple of years previously. It was only on sale in the States however and had to a large extent bombed. It never sold well, was withdrawn from sale in 1974 and never even made it as far as our shores. In contrast, its replacement, the CB400F, become a hit before anyone had even ridden one, purely because of its looks. Honda had done a very clever design job; they had made a four-cylinder 408cc bike that looked to be no bigger than a 250. It had a café

In the mid-1960s the 450cc *'Black Bomber'* was a highly exotic, desirable motorcycle. By the mid-1970s, its progeny, the CB500T was not. Slow, vibratory and bland it was amazing Honda sold any at all - though obviously I couldn't say this in my write-up

racer look about it too, accentuated by four, sinuous, swooping exhaust pipes, which fed into a single right-side silencer. You've probably picked-up that I'm not a great lover of fours, but the littlest Honda was a different kettle of fish entirely. For a start it was really fun to ride. It was light and flickable, unsurprisingly it was totally smooth and, if full use was made of its six-speed gearbox and 37bhp engine, it could really fly. The engine needed to be revved hard but it coped admirably with a thrashing, the tacho needle rarely being very far from the red line.

Obviously, this didn't make for a relaxing ride, but this didn't bother most. The 400/4 sold in huge numbers in the UK and, after riding the test bike, my colleague Bob Edwards bought one too. On my recommendation he had previously bought a Yamaha DT175, but the 400 suited him more. It was a jack-of-all-trades and Steve Murray, Bill Smith's workshop foreman, proved its speed and reliability by finishing twelfth in the 500cc class of the 1976 Production TT. He averaged nearly 90mph and passed many machines racing in the 1000cc class along the way. I knew all this as on one of my frequent visits to Bill Smith's I was collared by Steve and received a blow-by-blow account. His story must have lasted as long as the race, so it made me laugh when I heard his epitaph years later: *'Steve loved motorbikes and he loved to talk!'*

The final bike I tested in 1975 was also sold as a middleweight, but most wouldn't have classified it as such. In comparison with the others, it was quite portly, didn't have the same image and wouldn't have appealed to the same demographic at all; it was the BMW R60/6. It was essentially the same size and weight as its bigger stable-mates so, in comparison, I thought it would be underpowered and a bit basic. In the latter case this was certainly true of the antiquated front drum brake and, at £1,399, for that reason alone, many would have dismissed it out of hand. It was also true that the R60/6 didn't have the same get-up-and-go of the bigger flat twins, but it had a charm all of its own and it could easily have satisfied the riding needs of many. The bigger-is-better buying public didn't agree with me though and the 600 was soon dropped from BMW's range.

It was a shame. On the day that Jeremy was due to collect the bike, Steff rode it from our home in North Wales into Chester, much to the surprise of some of my colleagues. They didn't think that a girl could ride a big bike, but both she and the R60 showed them what a practical all-rounder it made. Incidentally if you asked me now what my own favourite bike from this group of middleweights would be, my answer would be the same as in 1975: the BMW. It just suited my style of riding: fuss-free, comfortable and relaxed. One of my pet hobby horses at the time was that manufacturers didn't really build top quality middleweights and I thought the R60 was the nearest thing. Myself and BMW were wrong however, partly due to the horrendous price; everyone and their dog bought a Honda 400/4 and I couldn't really blame them. It was and remains a fabulous machine.

Looking back it's sometimes easy to forget quite what an impact the original Honda 400/4 had. The sweeping 4-into-1 exhaust system was, and still is, a masterpiece

Chapter 5
Donning Hi-Viz

The column in the Observer obviously raised my profile. Truthfully it was beyond what it should have been, but as a result, in the spring of 1975, I got a phone call from Chester County Council's Road Safety Office. They asked if I'd be willing to call and see their Road Safety Officer, a chap called Len Williams, and I was, as his office was only five minutes' walk from the Observer's. I took an instant liking to the big, burly ex-policeman who met me, with his straightforward, practical style. It seemed he took to me too. We got on from the word go as he explained the idea in hand.

The school leaving age for non-academic students was being raised from fifteen to sixteen and a syllabus was being designed to provide more practical subjects in the extra year they had to study. As part of this the Road Safety Office had the idea of creating a twelve-week programme covering motorcycle maintenance and basic riding skills. Len said that the Road Safety Office and the Education Department had joined forces to purchase a Honda SS50 sports moped and this was to be used for the riding element: *'Would you consider teaching the riding and assisting with the maintenance courses?'*

I was surprised but genuinely interested and was pretty sure that the Observer would be too. It was a golden opportunity to promote the paper's local connections and commitments and the management saw it the same way as well. The paper loved the idea, so dates were agreed and I was once again in at the deep end; taking on something for which I had absolutely no qualifications. I had no previous teaching experience and there were no existing training schemes for me to copy: they'd not start appearing for at least another decade. I cobbled together a basic programme for the riding lessons however, based on what I'd learned through the school of hard knocks, as we all did back then. I shared this with Len, who thought that it looked great, so on the appointed day I turned up at Blacon High School, where I was surprised to be met by my old Geography teacher, whom I'd been taught by at another school. He would be supervising the boys on the course as despite the school being coeducational, and as a sign of the times I suppose, no girls had chosen to join.

As such there were a group of about ten teenage boys, clad in the ubiquitous green parkas and flares who, although clearly eager to learn, were equally intent to put one over each other by trying to give the impression that they could all ride bikes already. I was surprised how they addressed the teacher too: quite informally. When he'd taught us, nobody spoke unless they were spoken to. It was obviously all change in the 1970s and I wondered how the lads would behave on the course. On this I initially showed them the main features of the bike, explaining the controls and their correct function. Most of them were quite attentive, though their questions showed that their level of understanding wasn't as comprehensive as they had implied. A couple of lads started chatting when I was explaining the controls, so I stopped and told them that they could pay attention or leave, it was all the same to me. That, off-the-cuff comment, did all that it needed to do. The boys really did want to be involved, there was rarely anything but full attention from then on.

When it came to riding I demonstrated starting the Honda, engaging first gear and feeling the clutch to its *biting point* before being able to move off. The students' faces told me that they thought this would be child's play, but when it came to their turn, none managed a smooth take-off without several abortive attempts first. It's second nature when you know how to do it, we all do, but easier to do than explain; a bit like…..riding a bike. This experience brought them back down to earth a bit and they started to take things more seriously from then on, all wanting to become better riders than their friends. By the end of the course, they could all start a bike, move off smoothly, change gear, brake and ride around a set of cones on the school playground. It was entirely successful and the Road Safety and Education Departments must have agreed. They asked me to repeat the course at another school on the other side of the city. Though it amuses me today to remember that there was no risk assessment, no parental permission sort and no insurance arranged. In those days, you just *did* things in an environment which would seem totally alien today. They'd all learnt to ride a bike however and it looked like I was able to teach.

With the Honda 500T I had managed to get around the quandary of dealing with a lemon of a test bike through a little literary ambiguity. Thankfully that wasn't necessary with the next problem bike I rode, as I never got to write it up at all. It was a shame though the way it turned out, as it could have opened up a whole new chapter, testing a very appealing range of machines. At the time Coburn & Hughes were the Ducati and Moto Guzzi concessionaires and they would soon add Benelli. They supported their sales drive through a high-profile and presumably very costly advertising campaign featuring as many scantily clad women as motorcycles. Tom Loughridge was persuaded to take on the agency for both brands and as a result asked me if I wanted to test his newest demonstrator, the Moto Guzzi 850cc T3. I suppose you'd call the T3 the base model in the range, as other variants, such as the California, S3 and the Automatic - remember that brief fad? – came in higher spec. with fairings, panniers and other accessories fitted as standard. I was really interested to see how this transverse, shaft-drive V-twin stacked up against the BMW R90 in particular, as they seemed obvious rivals. My first impressions were favourable; the engine was strong and very torquey and the handling for a big 535lb bike was really good. The T3 was never designed as an around town bike however so I was looking forward to a ride down to Derbyshire to give the bike a proper shakedown and longer test.

On this, the Guzzi felt very similar to the BMWs in many ways. The engine was perhaps a little less refined, but it certainly covered the miles quickly and effortlessly on my rapid ride down. However, when quite close to my destination I stopped at a set of traffic lights and happened to glance down at the front of the bike. To my horror, I saw a great deal of fluid all over the forks, which was heading towards the disc brakes. I pulled over to the side of the road to find that one of the fork seals had failed. It had somehow popped out of its housing, damaging itself in the process, with the pumping action of the forks doing a great job in distributing the oil all over the bike.

Luckily, I had a rag with me so I wiped the oil off as well as I could, but no amount of fiddling could persuade the seal back into place. I continued my journey, slowly, periodically stopping to wipe oil off at regular intervals, until eventually there was no more left to come out. From then on I didn't have to keep stopping, but I rode home very steadily, as obviously the bike now had only half the damping. The next day, I returned the Guzzi to Tom's and he was horrified. Horrified but perhaps not totally surprised.

Within a week, Tom phoned me to say that he had received more warranty claims with Guzzi and Ducati in a month than he had ever had with any of the Japanese brands, or indeed with his Laverdas. Added to this, the support he was getting from the importers was less than satisfactory. Fearing that the excellent reputation that he had built up for after sales service would be compromised, Tom cancelled his franchise and rapidly sold on his outstanding Ducati and Moto

The entire Moto Guzzi range was beautiful, though the beauty only went skin deep. I could have tested the lot, but Tom Loughridge turned down the concession and I couldn't really blame him. He was happy with his Laverdas

Guzzi stock. Understandably, he asked me not to publish a test of the T3 though in many ways I was disappointed. I'd liked the bike and it clearly had great potential. In their looks the mid-70s were a stylistic high point for both Guzzi and Ducati, though mechanically it was clearly very different. I fully understood Tom's decision. From a business perspective it made total sense and I was compensated for the disappointment with the offer of probably the most exotic and charismatic motorcycle on the road: a Laverda 1000 3C.

Nowadays everyone talks about *Jotas*, but it was a year or so before that name was applied. Until then, this was the highest performance model Laverda made and, having enjoyed the 750 twin, I was ecstatic at the chance to ride the 981cc, 85bhp triple. Like most, I'd only ever seen pictures of the bike and like its stable-mate it looked as if it had been hewn out of solid metal compared with the rather *bitty* multis offered by other manufacturers. The pictures didn't prepare me for seeing the Laverda in the flesh for the first time though; it was beautiful, but an absolute monster. At 495lb it was actually lighter than the 750 twin, but the 3C was very tall and on it, at slow speed, I felt very precarious. However when I'd nervously pressed the starter button, I was greeted by an incredible, thunderous sound. Triples have a music all of their own and this bike could certainly play a great tune, even at a standstill. It's also worth remembering here quite what an impact these Superbikes of the 1970s had. There's been nothing really since, which has created the same excitement. To an audience fed on leaking, rehashed British twins year-after-year, machines like the Laverda seemed to come from a different planet. When they were announced there was a lot of, *'Oh, that'll never happen'* so to actually see them - and hear them - in the flesh had a jaw-dropping effect, even on the most experienced.

I wouldn't say I was overawed by the prospect of the Laverda, but riding the big triple certainly proved a mixed bag. I can't remember the adverts at the time exactly, but they were all about being, *'A man's bike'* and, with its heavy clutch and slow steering, town riding certainly suited a gorilla's physique: it wasn't much fun. Even on the open road the engine felt quite lumpy, but if the throttle was wound open, the bike took off and finally felt like it was in its element. This was the fastest bike that I had ridden up to this point and I became acutely aware that I wasn't really up to the job: I wasn't a good enough rider. If I had been, my licence wouldn't have lasted very long. In many ways, I loved the big Laverda but in the cold light of day it was simply too much for me. Though interestingly enough, Tony Barrow rode the triple and, as a fearless racer – he was Allan Steele's passenger after all - he wrung its neck and loved it. He was still raving about the big Laverda when I met him thirty years later: it wasn't a bike you easily forgot.

I had several opportunities to ride Laverda triples subsequently and I got to grips with the fact that they only really started to make sense at very high speeds. Pete *PK* Davies and Roger Winterburn dominated production racing in the UK on them, but they were made of sterner stuff. I preferred touring bikes and Suzuki, through Dugdale Motors, soon had the ideal thing for me. Suzuki's flagship at the time, was technically very interesting. The GT750, water-cooled triple was introduced in 1971, when Suzuki went down a different route to all

I'm not sure if any other motorcycle, before or since, has quite matched the physical presence of Laverda's triple. They were awe-inspiring at the time of their release, and still look like mobile pieces of art today. Too big for me though

their competitors. They decided not to conform to the four-cylinder, four-stroke format, instead plumping for an advanced two-stroke tourer, even if by the time that I tested the bike the writing was on the wall: emission laws and rising petrol prices made big two-strokes untenable. Suzuki did briefly flirt with Wankel technology and I kick myself now, as Tom Loughridge had one and I never asked for a ride. In many ways it was more of the same though, as eventually Suzuki caved in and followed the four-stroke trend. As a one-off piece of history, the GT750 *'Kettle'* was unusual and unique therefore. Parked up, a Kettle would attract more attention than any other machine on the road, with the engine undoubtedly the talking point. Developed from the proven technology of the twin-cylinder GT500 – which itself was derived from the TS250 single - the 750 triple was smooth, extremely quiet, tractable and, at 70bhp, impressively powerful. In its racing form, the TR750 proved successful at National and World Championship level, particularly in the hands of Barry Sheene, but on the road the GT had been dubbed the *'Flexi-flyer'*. This was due to its wayward handling, so while superficially similar to the racer the road bike actually had some different DNA. This was particularly the case with the engine. The road bike could undoubtedly be hustled through the gears, to reach a decent velocity, but a lot of people spent much money trying - unsuccessfully - to make GTs perform like Barry's. The road-going GT750 actually encouraged a far steadier approach. At 482lb, it was quite heavy, but once up to speed the weight wasn't too noticeable and I admired Suzuki's unconventional approach to Superbike design. My test concluded that it would make a tireless touring mount, but would I have bought one with my own money? Well, like many riders at the time, I was conservative with a small 'c' and it was perhaps just too different for me.

Interestingly enough, today the Kettle has a thriving, cult following. Bikes fetch very good money and as an aside on big money bikes, you might note one obvious omission: Kawasaki. I did actually ride several *Big Zeds*, as my cousin's husband owned a Z1000 and a work friend had a Z1-R. My brief acquaintances showed that they were very well engineered and could easily hold their own with any of their contemporaries, to the point that they were possibly better. However, they never featured in my tests for one simple reason. There were no Kawasaki dealers in the area and the purpose of my column - as far as the management of the newspaper were concerned – was to trigger dealer advertising. Talking up a bike which wasn't available from one of our local dealers was hardly going to help mine or the Observer's position, particularly as there were a growing number of dealers actively offering support. My focus had to be on the machines that those dealers were selling.

One of these dealers was Alan Dugdale, of Hector Dugdale Motors, who was a big help in providing bikes to road test for one particular reason: he was seriously competitive. Alan always wanted to be one step ahead of the other dealers and would take every opportunity to get one over on them. He hated it if he felt someone else was getting the upper hand and, while Alan never actually said anything to me, I knew that he resented the publicity that Tom Loughridge received from my track test of his racer. As such I was grateful when he came up with an appropriate reposte.

Upstaging Tom must have been on his mind as, one day in the autumn of 1975, he rang me up to tell me of an *exclusive*. I took this with a pinch of salt, as Alan's promises didn't always materialise. I wasn't aware of him selling anything out of the ordinary, but sure enough, he was as good as his word. I was bowled over, *'Would you like to ride a TT winner?'* It was the Honda CB500 four that Charlie Williams and Eddie Roberts had won the 500cc Production TT on, just a few months previously. There were a few more surprises though, as when I asked Alan if he had booked a track session I was left a little shocked by his reply, *'No, we'll just bung the trade plate on it and you can have it on the road for a week or so.'* I thought, *'Hold on, is this legal?'* But Alan dismissed my concerns out of hand, *'It's a production bike and if it can pass TT scrutineering as such the local constabulary can hardly make a hue and cry.'*

The year was ticking on by now and November wasn't the ideal month to have a TT-winning bike on the road. I wasn't complaining, but I had some trepidation and certainly felt some responsibility; can you imagine if I dropped the thing? Also, irrespective of what Alan said, I

Don't try this at home kids. U-turning the *'Dugdale's reposte'*, while on test - it didn't have much lock! I was always expecting to be stopped by the police while riding their Honda 500 Production racer but, amazingly, wasn't

fully expected to be stopped by the Police, as the thing hardly blended in. I wasn't going to look a gift horse in the mouth however and once on the road I couldn't help but compare the Honda with Tom Loughridge's Suzuki, which had led the same race: the experience put them poles apart. They were nothing like each other and probably the opposite of what most people would have expected. The Honda felt heavy and, with an ill-fitting fairing, bulky in comparison to the Suzuki. The riding position was also much less forgiving. Compared to the torquey Suzuki the power was all at the top end of the rev band, though if the motor was kept there, it was undeniably very fast: too fast for the public roads. I could only admire Charlie and Eddie's ability to get the best out of the Honda as I found it hard to ride. Being professional racers I presumed they'd think otherwise, preferring a peaky rev-happy engine, but years later Charlie told me that neither he

A photo I took of John Williams at the TT in 1976. He was seventh in the Senior race but won the Classic. At the end of 1975 I didn't know I'd soon be interviewing him

nor Eddie liked it. They only completed the minimum practice in order to qualify and they actually had no expectations. It was a TT winner none the less and, as I was an occasional visitor to the local Wheelwright's Motorcycle Club, at Elton, near Ellesmere Port, I arranged to take the bike for members to have a closer look. The day of the meeting it was cold and wet, but a promise is a promise, so off I set to meet the two - yes two - people who had turned up! It was a bit disappointing, particularly as that was my last ride of the year, a year which had been pretty remarkable. Twelve months previously I would hardly have dared for such experiences, but moving on I also knew I now needed to add a bit more variety, to take my column up a notch.

Chapter 6
The Novice Interviewer

I couldn't fill every column inch with road tests, particularly during the depths of winter. The winter was always a bit of a famine period when little was going on other than trials. It was hard to get readers excited about road riding, but I had a plan. The North West was a hotbed of racing activity in the 1970s so I lined up a number of local stars. Among these I particularly remember arranging to meet Charlie Williams, who was already a multiple TT winner and had I think nine podiums under his belt at the time. I met him at Dugdale's, early in 1975, in the run-up to that year's TT, where he very patiently went through his plans for the year ahead and talked me around his Dugdale-sponsored, Maxton-framed machines: all Yamahas. I was somewhat star-struck at meeting a genuine celebrity TT racer and my interview skills were not exactly finely honed. I managed to cobble something together however and Charlie was pleased with what I penned. It was a good start and, while I missed Stan Woods somehow, that same year I interviewed Bill Smith, Eddie Roberts and Steve Murray. Again, it was primarily about their TT plans, as we are very close to the ferry up here in Cheshire and the TT holds a special affection for spectators and riders alike. In each case reasonable, if not headline grabbing, pieces went into the paper, cementing the column's credentials for local content. The following year I travelled to Great Sutton, on the Wirral, to interview ex-British Sidecar Champion Bill Currie, about his intention to come out of retirement. He did race again, and how. He was still racing at his beloved TT up to 2010 and beyond.

Over the winter I was also introduced to Suzuki GB rider, John Williams, who kindly invited me to his house in Heswall, not far from me. I was quite surprised to find such a famous rider living in such an ordinary, semi-detached house, but then the money-side of racing was still a mystery to me. As Barry Sheene and Phil Read drove Rolls-Royces, it seemed reasonable - in my ignorance - to expect that their rivals might be paid similarly. How wrong could I be? I was offered tea and biscuits by John and his wife and John turned out to be a very modest guy. He carried the mantle of a star lightly and was quite matter of fact about his considerable successes. He seemed in no hurry for me to leave, and, though what I wrote was probably quite superficial, he seemed pleased when I took a copy over the following week for him to read. Later I got to know John better as I would see him quite regularly. I thought he was going places, one to watch.

I was passionate about road racing and as well as John I followed particularly the exploits of Charlie Williams, Stan Woods, Eddie Roberts, Bill Smith, Steve Murray, Derek Huxley and, of course, Allen Steele. I would work race reports in to my column as often as possible and I soon found out that if I wrote a polite letter on the Observer's headed notepaper, a couple of free 'Press' tickets for events would magically appear. Armed with these, I then discovered that if I went to the Press Office on arrival, I would be given a Press armband that would give me trackside access and a seat in the grandstand Press Box. Needless to say, I covered every motorcycle meeting from then on, combing the paddock for stories and taking my own trackside photographs. I became an established feature and particularly remember one year at the Oulton Park Transatlantic round that the famous journalist Chris Carter, who wrote for Motor Cycle among other publications, quizzed me about what was going on. He borrowed most of my notes as he'd completely missed one of the main Match Races. It seemed he'd lost all track of time, when he went for some *refreshments*.

It was illuminating to mix with such personalities, as it wasn't just racers I interviewed. There were many interesting characters off the track too, among whom I got to interview Ron Williams, the man behind Maxton Engineering. In his Cheshire workshop, Ron hand-crafted frames for Yamaha race bikes primarily and built these into complete rolling chassis. Maxtons handled significantly better than a standard Yamaha and Ron's frames were, and still are, in high demand. Ron was a quiet but clearly very thoughtful engineer. He'd come up through the ranks of Formula One car building where he had learned a thing or two about suspension in particular. Without giving away any hard won secrets, Ron explained to me how his frames differed from the standard items and I was privileged to be able to watch him set up his jigs to actually create one in front of my very own eyes. As with many talented artisans he made it look very easy, his actions demonstrating far better than words. It was a wonder to watch a craftsman at work and one thing - that I learned later – which really impressed me was that if Ron didn't like a rider he'd simply refuse to build them a frame, regardless of how much money they might offer. He did build quite a lot however, as the list of riders who achieved success riding his products has proved.

We had an engaging, enlightening discussion, so I had plenty for an article. However, before I left Ron's workshop, he said to me in a conspiratorial tone, *'If I show you a secret project that I will be working on, will you promise not to publish anything about it?'* He led me to a corner of the workshop where there was a bulky item on the floor. I hadn't really noticed it before, but when he lifted the tarpaulin covering it, it revealed what I recognised immediately as a works Honda NR500 Grand Prix engine. Such was Ron's international reputation that this engine - the legendary *'Nearly Ready'* - had been sent in great secrecy, for Ron to build a frame around. Honda had failed with their monocoque, *'clam shell'* chassis, so they went to Ron without a second thought and were sufficiently impressed with his handiwork to employ him as a consultant for some years to come. As I said, a very talented man, who gave me an insight into a fascinating and little-understood part of the racing game.

Looking back, if I have one regret during this period, it was that I missed out on the chance to write a great article about a pioneer of women's motorcycle sport as, through lack of preparation and research, I fluffed it. I discovered that an old lady who lived in the area had been involved in some way in motorcycle sport, in the 1920s and 1930s. Her name was Marjorie Cottle and when I called round the frail old lady who answered the door didn't fit my mental image of how a successful motorcycle competitor should look. However, over tea and cakes, she recounted tales of riding in pre-war competition on a variety of machines, both home and abroad. Marjorie was so self-effacing that I didn't really take in what an exceptional rider she had been, nor the magnitude of her successes. I should have known from the glint in her eye when she told me of her exploits that she had been something special. So, inevitably, I wrote what I now consider to be a cringingly scant account of her life: I did her a great disservice. Partly to set the record straight, it's worth recording here a few of Marjorie's achievements. She was a works rider for Raleigh in the 1920s, being successful in numerous trials. From 1925 until 1939, she competed in the world's toughest motorcycling event, the International Six Days Trial (ISDT) gaining a prestigious Gold Medal on no less than eight occasions. All in all, Marjorie was an exceptional sporting motor-cyclist who could compete with the toughest and most talented of men, entirely on equal terms, when those terms were loaded against her. I wish I could have done her justice, as her escape from the 1939 ISDT event in Austria alone, as war was being declared, is worthy of a feature film in its own right. The Sound of Music, on motorbikes.

My respect for Marjorie Cottle only grew when the opportunity arose to test a vintage motorcycle of her era. I was offered a 1928 Rudge Whitworth Sports Special and I thought it would make a great, left-field road test, during a period before the term 'Classic' had even been coined. It was a machine which had twice won its class at the Isle of Man Rudge Rally so, while I was obviously a bit apprehensive about riding such a valuable machine, the question that was actually uppermost in my mind was, 'Will I be able to start it?' The bike had an abundance of levers and unfamiliar controls, as in addition to the familiar ones there was an ignition advance/retard lever, an air lever, oil tap, valve-lifter and, strangest of them all to me, a hand gear-change. The bike was also equipped with linked brakes and girder front forks, so I had a lot to take in before I even got started. You might be surprised that I was bamboozled by such stuff having owned old British bikes myself but, save for the lack of a kick-start, the layout of today's bikes is no different to what I grew up with; it's all been the same since the early 1960s.

It was quite an education, as I was shown the correct positions for the air and advance/retard controls, both for starting and for normal

A big picture for a big omission. Works Suzuki rider Stan Woods was a big part of the local racing scene but for the life of me I can find no evidence that I ever published an interview with him in Motorcycle Scene. Apologies Stan. Here he is admiring Eddie Roberts' Dugdale Yamaha riding, while at the same being demonstrated how to change gear by hand on the move. *'The trick is to not rush things'* were the owner's final words as I sat astride the bike and, with the use of the valve-lifter, I swung the engine over compression and then, with one hefty kick, brought the big single into life. It had quite a throaty roar, at odds with its refined looks, but as I cautiously engaged first gear it set off remarkably smoothly. I hoped that no one could see my fumbling attempt at finding second gear, but somehow I managed it, wobbling all over the road. In many ways it was like learning to ride all over again as most of the controls were unfamiliar. The gear change pattern was back for first and forward for the rest, though one big advantage of the hand change was that I could tell what gear I was in, just by looking down; I could work out what gear I was in from the position the lever sat in, in the notches of the *'gate'*. Once in top I could relax a little and enjoy the bike, as there was certainly no lack of power. The little Rudge was very light, feather-weight compared with any contemporary machine, and there was plenty of grunt from its high-compression four-valve engine. It got up to speed quite rapidly and, surprisingly, the girder forks and rigid rear-end threw up no surprises, as long as potholes were avoided. The linked brakes also worked far better than I had expected and I found that on the quiet roads around Chirk, where I was testing it, it proved to be an entirely practical machine.

Following this initial jaunt I was generously loaned the bike for a week and, as I got used to its idiosyncrasies, my respect for the little Rudge only grew. Overcrowded urban roads were obviously best avoided, but on the open road it coped admirably with modern traffic; it was easily able to keep pace. As such when I returned the bike the following Saturday, while relieved to deliver it in one piece I felt genuinely privileged to have experienced such a window into motorcycling's past, though one aspect of the machine was thoroughly modern.

There's an adage that there's nothing new in motorcycling, it's all been done before. The Rudge's radial four-valve head was a case in point, as it had only recently been reported in the press that with the XS500 it had just been *'discovered'* by the Japanese. I'd already experienced this phenomenon before however, as when I'd tested the Suzuki GT750 there was much talk of, *'The world's first water-cooled production bike'*, a claim which had retired brigadiers spluttering into their beer. *Everyone* knew that Scott had done it first, before the First World War, building such a machine not twenty-five miles from my present house. What was less well known was that you could still buy a new one - well the latest incarnation - the glorious, Derby-built, 700cc Silk. I know, because I rode one.

This was outside my usual testing routine of obtaining local machines and came about through the enquiries of a Wheelwrights Motorcycle Club member, Keith Wilkinson. He was genuinely interested in the new Silk but knew he'd never get a test ride on such an exotic and rare machine. However, he asked me if I could ask for a ride, presuming that the Cheshire Observer might have sufficient clout. I wasn't very hopeful. I left it down to Keith to make the approach so was very pleased when the response came back in the affirmative, with a factory visit thrown in for free. It was agreed that he and another club stalwart, Dennis Carter-Wardell, would tag along for the experience, both hopeful of cadging a test ride too. We set out for Derbyshire one sunny morning: Dennis on his BMW sidecar outfit, Keith on a Suzuki GT500 and myself on the previously mentioned 850 Guzzi, complete with leaky forks.

To be honest, I knew very little about the Silk before our visit, other than that its engine was based on the vintage water-cooled, Scott, two-stroke twin. This was a peculiarly British curiosity which had remained largely unchanged throughout its production life, which ran from the pre-WWI period to about 1962. I couldn't really imagine how this could make for a viable modern motorcycle, but I was intrigued. Hopefully it was more advanced than their building, as when we eventually arrived at their home in Darley Abbey we were met by what looked like an old mill, reached by crossing a little toll bridge. It was more 17th than 20th century and more cottage than cottage industry. Once inside the curious *factory*, we were introduced to George Silk and his partner Maurice Patey. George looked exactly like what he was: a young enthusiastic engineer. Maurice on the other-hand was the image of the well-spoken aristocratic gentleman and the epitome of what I expected a Scott rider to be. They were quite an unlikely pairing.

Over a welcome cup of tea, we were given a potted history of the company which was founded in 1970, when George started building the 'Silk Scott Special'. This was essentially a Spondon 125cc - yes *125cc* - rolling chassis fitted with an improved, but still vintage, Scott engine. Between 1971 and 1975, twenty one Silk Scott Specials were built, with the limiting factors to expansion being the short supply of Scott engines and the owner of the Scott name refusing to allow any more new engines to be built. Undeterred George and David Midgelow, a Rolls-Royce engineer, designed and built a new 698cc power unit, although still along original Scott lines. They were helped with the porting of the engine by famous two-stroke expert Dr. Gordon Blair, of Queen's University Belfast (QEB), and by Spondon Engineering, into whose 125cc Grand Prix chassis the Silk 700S engine was shoehorned. As anyone with a modicum of knowledge would appreciate, the names, Spondon, Rolls-Royce and QEB were globally renowned, so while the Silk was the product of classic British garden shed engineering the concept was very sound.

To my eyes, the bike looked quintessentially English: an eye-catching mix of ancient and modern. The frame and forks gave the Silk the look of a modern lightweight racer, whilst the engine, unsurprisingly, was reminiscent of an old Scott. The only obvious update to my untrained eye was the use of a Velocette gearbox, though Velocette of course was also now long since dead. First impressions when sitting on the bike were really positive. I couldn't believe how small, light and slim it was, feeling to me about the same size as the Yamaha 200 that I had once owned. The 700S started first kick, to a meaty burble, and I set off watched by the little crowd, out of the courtyard, over the bridge and onto a suggested route that had been outlined to me in advance.

The Silk was simplicity itself to ride at slow speeds. It seemingly had no power band, it was like a little diesel, and with its light weight changing direction was effortless. Once out of the 30mph limit, I opened the throttle and the soundtrack subtly changed however. No, let's be honest, there was no subtlety about it. The noise went from a subdued, civilised, burble to a screaming howl: there's good reason why the Scott Owners Club magazine is called simply, *'Yowl.'* The bike took off like a scalded cat once given its head and, had I done my research in advance, I would have realised that 48bhp from a bike weighing a mere 309lbs - that's *less* than a Japanese 250 - would make for strong acceleration. Amazingly, the maximum power was also produced at a lowly 6,000rpm whilst the tractability was explained by peak torque being produced an incredible 3,000 revs lower. It made for an extraordinary riding experience and I was soon arriving at bends much sooner than I had anticipated. I needn't have worried though, the brakes were brilliant and the cornering exceptional. The Silk chassis showed its racing pedigree with exemplary steering and suspension, while the brakes showed their worth when I came around a blind bend - at slightly illegal speed - to be confronted by two policemen sitting by a trestle table at the side of the road. I'd never seen a speed camera before, but I was sure this was what the array of

A Silk I photographed later in 1976 at the Racing & Sports Show. This was the SPR, the Production racer, a type ridden by Alan Jackson and Dave Roper among others

electronics on the table was. So, I hauled on the brakes and the bike lost 30mph in an instant; I rode past the scowling constables at a perfectly legal speed.

When I got back to the factory both George Silk and Maurice Patey were genuinely interested in my feedback. Dennis and Keith were also allowed their hoped-for rides and they came back just as impressed as me. I had a new bike to add to my list of favourites, but of course I could never have afforded to buy one. At £1,355 it was one of the most expensive machines available, the reasons for which soon became glaringly obvious. Before heading home we were treated to a tour of the factory which was a small-scale, artisanal operation. The handful of workers employed each had a single bike on their bench which they painstakingly hand-built, slowly, on a one by one basis.

It was odd, but rather than being elated by such an exceptional bike I left Silk Engineering in a really quite depressed state of mind. I had ridden a wonderful motorcycle, but I would never be able to afford one and on a business level the enterprise was clearly doomed to fail. Silk needed the resources of a major British manufacturer behind them and of course there were no British manufacturers left. It took me a long time to get over that feeling, not helped by the long, halting, ride home. The contrast between the heavy, ailing Guzzi and the lithe Silk couldn't have been any more stark. With the British industry it always seemed to be a case of, *'Oh dear, what could have been?'* Such a shame, I would have gladly sold a kidney for a Silk.

Chapter 7
Off-Roading a Commando

Although I was selling advertising, testing bikes, riding trails and setting up home I was still in contact with the Road Safety Office. Primarily this was over setting-up future schools courses but it paid dividends when, through them, I got an offer from the local police. It was still hard to believe but my name was in the public domain and I'd somehow become the local face of motorcycling; the police thought I could give *them* some publicity. *'Would you be interested in coming down to the Police Driver Training Headquarters to go through an abbreviated version of the Police Motorcyclist training course?'* The idea was that I could then write up my experiences for my column, which was a no-brainer for the management of the Observer. Before I had time to even work through the implications the paper agreed, the deal was done, *'Oh well, why not?'*

I was expecting a Chief Instructor to be quite officious, but from the start Bill Ward was all smiles and informality, giving me the impression that although the day might be hard, it would also be fun. He took me to a classroom to explain the basics of the programme and the first thing that surprised me was that they actually preferred non-riders as recruits: *'They have no bad habits to un-learn.'* Thinking that I'd probably have quite a lot to unlearn, Bill explained that we would start out with him following me, to assess my riding and, if he was happy, we would then go on to do some high-speed work. I realised that the only assessment I'd ever undergone previously was riding around the block a few times, largely unobserved, as that was to pass my bike test. As, let's be honest, it was hardly rigorous back in the day. As such, I wasn't sure how I would cope, let alone score, so I set my ambitions low; my target was not to embarrass myself.

I was allocated a Training School BMW R75 for the day and fitted with a two-way radio. That was so we could communicate on the ride, where we'd be joined by another sergeant, on a police spec. Triumph 500. It was handy having the BMW, as it was a bike with which I was now quite familiar, and handy having a radio too: this was space technology for a layman. With Bill's directions magically reaching my ear, I didn't have to worry about getting lost, I could just concentrate on the riding. We did this for about an hour, on a mixture of urban and open roads, and aware of an experienced police instructor close behind me, I concentrated like never before.

Via the radio Bill encouraged me as we went along, making suggestions relating mainly to road positioning and signalling, and when we stopped at a butty van his feedback was pretty positive. The one thing which stuck in my mind being that he told me I was indicating far too often, *'Only indicate if it will be useful to other road users.'* I was good enough to proceed to the high-speed element however, where Bill gave me the same instruction that he gave all his trainees, *'Obey 30mph and 40mph limits, but everywhere else, make good progress.'* Which essentially meant, ride as fast as I could whilst remaining safe. Bill led us into the Cheshire countryside where I did my best to follow his lines and keep up, as he held speeds of 80mph to 90mph without break for miles. Bill's incredible observational skills were behind his ability, as he provided a running commentary throughout, describing hazards and road features in great detail. This was before the advent of speed cameras, so we were riding within the limits of safety, rather than the letter of the law. At one point, Bill overtook a car on the approach to a blind bend. I hung back, but the radio crackled, *'Nothing coming, you're safe to overtake.'* The car driver must have thought I had a death wish, but when we stopped again, for a debrief, Bill emphasised how the use of the police's COP system (Concentration, Observation and Planning) enabled safe high speed riding of that sort. It might look dangerous, but it wasn't, *'You don't take risks, you make judgements based on observation.'*

To be honest I'd forgotten about the other rider, but at this point he caught up on his Triumph which, from the ominous sounds coming from its engine, hadn't enjoyed the high speed work. It was only a 500 after all and he wisely decided to return to base as the Triumph was clearly feeling the strain. As he rode off I felt for the poor mechanic who would inevitably have to strip the tired engine down, though I didn't have long to dwell on it. Bill was, *'Right, I'll give you directions well in advance, so you only have to concentrate on your riding. Your time to lead.'* He also asked me to give him a running commentary on the ride i.e. *'Junction coming up on the left, red van waiting to turn right'* and the like. I found that this actually helped, though obviously not enough. At one stage, we were cracking on a bit around a left-hander and I became aware of Bill exhorting me to, *'Get it leant over more'* as he came up, riding alongside. It's not often that you get a policeman telling you to go faster when you're already breaking the law.

When we eventually arrived back at Police H.Q. in Crewe, Bill gave me an extensive debrief. He was surprisingly complimentary and said that apart from one part - the high speed pursuit element of the course - we had completed an entire assessment to Police Class 1. I had achieved a pass and he even presented me with a certificate. I was chuffed, not least as the endorsement meant I'd probably been underplaying my test riding skills. There was a humorous postscript to the day too. A few weeks later Bill rang again, to see if I was interested in the off-road element of the course.

Now here, obviously, I was in my element, though I was curious when they told me, *'Your own bike won't be necessary, we'll supply an appropriate machine.'* I wondered at the time, *'What sort of off-roaders do Cheshire Police ride?'* On the agreed day, I drove to a rendezvous point out in the sticks and then followed Bill to the *'track'*. This turned out to be a muddy field, with a wooded section at one end and my *'off-road bike'* in the middle. It was a high-mileage, ex-patrol, Norton Commando, complete with fairing and worn out TT 100 triangular tyres. *'Are you joking?'*

'No' was the answer. Bill explained that Police motorcyclists would need to continue a pursuit off-road if necessary and obviously they wouldn't be able to stop to change bikes. *'Fair enough'* I thought, so I followed Bill who soon built up a head of steam. Despite the seeming unsuitability of the bike, my green lane riding skills kicked in and I was soon standing on the footrests and solely using the back brake to slow down. The Norton was way bigger than anything I'd ridden off-

road before, but by using my normal approach I was able to keep up without too many problems: other than the flying mud. I realised that Bill was doing his best to cover me, so dodged as much as possible and when we eventually stopped, Bill turned to me with a big grin on his face, *'You've done this before, haven't you?'* We had a good laugh, as besides being a confident rider and authoritative teacher, he had a well developed sense of humour. The training had been really interesting and while it wasn't the last I'd be seeing of Bill, as the winter was coming to an end, my focus was now in a different direction.

The Observer would not be sponsoring Allen Steele in 1976. It was always very clear that the support was a one-off arrangement, to get the team started, but it was a shame none the less. It didn't matter to me personally however, as I'd become friends with Allen and fully intended to go to as many meetings as I could during the season. Allen had been happy with how the first year had gone, but he also wanted to be more competitive. The BSA engine had always been to test the water. The perennial problem of course was that the available money did not match Allen's ultimate ambitions. Even so, he heard of an outfit that could take him to the next rung of the ladder, so that was the way to go: step-by-step. Local brothers Paul and Vince Biggs had an outfit for sale, powered by a Weslake engine. This power plant was an interesting story in itself. The Weslake engine was basically a Triumph twin with an eight-valve cylinder-head bolted on. It was developed for better breathing by the famous Rickman brothers in 1968 as while the Triumph company had an interest in it, it wasn't until 1982's TSS model that they got round to actually fitting one themselves. The company was continually in financial straits and by the early 1980s poor old Triumph was pretty much on the rocks.

During the intervening years, independently, both Weslake and Nourish produced their own eight-valve heads and marketed them for racing. The eight-valve top-ends proved very popular and the engine that Allen was looking at was built by Paul Biggs. Paul came from a big sidecar racing family – there are still Biggs racing today – and he was an excellent engineer. Indeed, he later became Stan Wood's mechanic, when Stan campaigned a private Suzuki RG500, after leaving Suzuki

Sidecar racers in the making? The Weslake at its first Oulton Park shakedown. In competition the driver and passenger would be substantially older

GB. Paul was always in demand for his ability to build fast, reliable engines, so it came as no surprise to discover that this Weslake engine was a bit special. It featured a Norton crankshaft and Paul's assembly was so precise that not a single gasket was used in the build. The deal clincher was that Paul agreed to look after the engine and that was why I found myself at a very cold Oulton Park, two days after Christmas, when Allen and Tony had their first trial outing. They were soon lapping significantly quicker than they had on the BSA. The engine still wouldn't be competitive against the big two-strokes that were slowly starting to appear on the grids, but over the season the Weslake held its own against the many four-cylinder, four-stroke powered outfits which were becoming the norm at club level. Allen and Tony rarely finished out of the top ten. Additionally, under the watchful eye of Paul Biggs, the Weslake was supremely reliable with only one retirement all year, due to a broken gear. That was important because, as privateers, they had to count every penny. They needed every bit of help they could get and I contributed through giving them plenty of coverage in the Observer, to the extent that I'd hear the odd moan and grumble that I talked about them to exclusion of all others. Was I biased? Too bloody right I was!

I think I maintained my objectivity in testing however and at the start on 1976 one of the first bikes I sampled was a Yamaha XS650, their four-stroke twin. The bike interested me as it was a head-on challenge to the big British twins, of which the aforementioned Triumph and Norton were the sole examples still standing. In my review I went into the comparison at some length, as to date the big parallel-twin was a uniquely British layout and this was Japan's first, direct, head-on challenge. The first version of the Yamaha reputedly had a good motor but evil handling. Poor handling was a characteristic of many Japanese machines of the time, but the Yamaha's was more evil than most. Percy Tait, an ex-Triumph test rider and racer of some repute, was drafted in to sort it out and found that while the handling was adequate on the smooth test track which Yamaha used at the time, he told the designers that it was different on British roads. He got them to create artificial bumps and undulations in the track and riding over these demonstrated to even the most sceptical observer the realities of the bike's flaws. Tait recommended significant frame bracing, a revised steering head angle and changes to the swinging arm.

It was the result of Tait's intervention, the XS650B, that I rode and it was no surprise that the Yamaha felt reminiscent of a Triumph Bonneville, just with the rough edges knocked off it. It had lost a little of the excitement, or maybe I should say character of Triumph's 360° crank in the transformation however, though I liked the unfussy overhead-cam engine a lot. In contrast to the other four-stroke Japanese bikes I'd ridden recently, it pulled really well from low revs and it was certainly a bit smoother than a Triumph, though not tremendously so, which was a bit of a disappointment. I was led to believe that what Yamaha had done with the crank removed vibration. It didn't, it just moved it elsewhere and made it....different. But what of the handling? Well, it wasn't a surprise to discover that the XS650 now had quite a taut, 'European' feel to it. There was none of the sogginess of Honda's fours, the ride being firm and precise. I really liked it. The XS had a real air of solidity and dependability about it and

I couldn't help feeling that the Yamaha was the bike that Triumph could have produced if the British industry hadn't been run by accountants. It was like the Silk all over again, a case of, *'Oh well, what could have been.'* I didn't say it at the time, it was taboo, but I would have chosen an XS650 over the current T140 Bonneville any day of the week.

Yamaha were rolling out a series of XS four-stroke machines at the time to complement and ultimately replace their two-stroke range, though we were oblivious to the latter. So, soon after, I took the opportunity to test the XS650's smaller stable-mate, the XS500. I borrowed it from the increasingly obliging Dugdale's and found it a more highly strung animal. I was expecting a scaled down version of the XS650 but with its newer, double-overhead-camshaft engine, featuring four valves per cylinder, it was clearly built to be revved, and had to be. Luckily though, Yamaha had fitted an *'Omni-Phase Balancer'* to reduce vibration at the high revs it both produced and required which proved very effective and made me wonder why it was absent from the vibratory XS650? It made the bike feel as smooth as a four and, being lighter than its big brother, the XS500 was more flickable and nimbler, making it in many ways feel more like one of Yamaha's smaller two-stroke twins. It was a competent bike but this XS didn't have an excess (excuse the pun) of character. I wasn't the only person who thought so either. The XS500 never sold well and was gone from the range within a couple of years. Yamaha didn't always get it right, though that couldn't be said of Dugdale's next offer: an RD400 two-stroke twin, as oh, what a rocketship.

I'm not sure if it was because I've always preferred tourers, or perhaps I was just growing up? But for whatever reason the RD400 was, if anything, actually far too frenetic for me. I still wasn't too old to appreciate the performance however. When full use of the throttle was made it was very hard to keep the front wheel on the floor, but this wasn't a criticism; this was a motorcycle that was designed to go quickly. I probably don't need to go over the history, but the RD series had a direct link back to Yamaha's, over-the-counter, GP racers and the 400's engine developed a healthy 44bhp. This, coupled to a light-weight race developed chassis, the same as the RD250's, made it a giant-killer. Riders used to more traditional British parallel twins would never have considered an RD, but they'd easily be humbled by one on the road. It was no surprise that RD400s totally dominated 500cc Production Racing. They could afford to give away 100cc and could still beat full 1,000cc machines. The RD400 was not for me however as it only seemed happy accelerating. I had no difficulty understanding why they were so popular though. They offered matchless performance and terrific value for money among the middleweight options. There was huge competition in this segment where Honda, surprisingly, had two very different bikes fighting for elbow room in a very congested market.

Now, you might say, *'Hold on, you only just tested two Honda 500s?'* That would be true, but things were moving tremendously fast in the mid-1970s and old models simply didn't last. Honda had two new and very different middleweight machines with which to tempt the buying public by 1976 and I was lucky enough to try them both. The first was Honda's CB550F2, which followed the CB550. Both were single-overhead-camshaft machines and they shared ninety-nine percent of their genes with the original CB500, CB400 and the CB750 fours. The first CB550 was in fact little more than an over-bored CB500, but 50bhp and a weight of 452lbs were quite respectable figures for a middleweight at that time. Unfortunately, the updated F2 generated little of the excitement of its smaller 400cc brother and the handling was sketchy, some would say vague. Reliability and smoothness were its strong points as it was rather characterless otherwise. I struggled for compliments at the time and in all honesty I can't really remember anything much about it now. But that counts for very little, the CB550 sold in large quantities: what did *I* know? By way of a contrast, Honda's other middleweight, the CX500, was a totally different proposition.

The *'Plastic Maggot'*, as the CX became affectionately known, was a real Marmite bike; you either loved it or hated it. Its bulbous appearance didn't help it and made you question whether Honda had a stylist at all. The CX looked anything but sporty, but it was certainly different: it had an 80°, transverse, V-twin, water-cooled engine, pushrod operated valve-gear and shaft-drive. In 1976 that was a lot to

The Yamaha RD400 was fast and furious. Cast wheels were pretty cool too. What more could you ask for? Nothing came close for the price

take in. The engine produced a competitive, if not mind blowing, 48bhp and the bike weighed 452lbs. That made it, on paper at least, a similar proposition to the CB550F2, though on first riding the CX500 I found it to be both top heavy and far too softly sprung. Even so, oddly, I liked it. It was very comfortable and in many ways it had a relaxed, loping, feel not dissimilar to a BMW: high praise from me. Indeed, it did become a bit of a poor man's BMW and quite rightly sold in large, no, huge numbers.

I admired what Honda did. They had gone out on a limb with something other than an in-line four and succeeded. I later knew many riders who positively gushed over their CX500s. Though, to its detriment, it wasn't without its flaws. Although my test machine was totally reliable, Honda had many problems with cam-chain tensioners in particular. A standard despatch rider joke - *every* despatch rider rode a CX500 - went along the lines of the following: *'Knock, knock.'*

'Who's there?' 'Honda cam-chain.' You see the chain and tensioner became virtual service parts and it took some time for Honda to fix the issue. Worse still the cam-chain was buried at the back of the bike, sandwiched between the engine and gearbox. This meant lifting the bike off the engine – yes, it was easier than doing it the other way around - splitting the engine and carrying out a whole load of other very messy work to change it. It was also regularly pointed out in the press, though not the Observer I hasten to add, that only Honda could put a cam-chain in a *pushrod* motor. I will nail my colours to the mast here though. I said, and still think, that the CX500 had real character. Some years later I was also exonerated somewhat as I was able to ride the CX650 Eurosport. This was a later development of the original bike, featuring mono-shock rear suspension, a bigger engine and *'European'* styling. It was a very impressive machine, as was the original 500, and as a result many were mercilessly ground into the road, over hundreds of thousands of miles. It's no surprise that good second-hand examples command very healthy prices today.

It was a busy time for testing but over the winter of 1975/6 Len Williams contacted me again over additional motorcycle training. Given the success of my courses in schools he wanted the scheme expanding to the general public. He'd already obtained the use of a classroom and playground, for six consecutive Saturday mornings, starting in April and wanted the course to be a mixture of theory and practical riding, open to anyone with a provisional licence. This sort of thing was new at the time, so Len asked me if I could publicise the course in my column. If so he said his department would pay for an accompanying advert, though I told him that this probably wouldn't be necessary; I could get local dealers to sponsor the page.

I thought that this was to be the limit of my involvement, but Len then blindsided me with an almost off-the-cuff request, *'I'd like you to be in charge of the practical, riding, element of the course.'* I hadn't seen that coming, but agreed anyway, thinking that I could deal with the practicalities later on. These would include the recruitment of a small team of instructors, who would be paid expenses and be under the Chief Instructor – me - responsible for running the whole thing.

The Honda CB550. Reading my test back it was full of generic platitudes as I struggled to find plus points. The best I could manage was to say that it was perfect for those for whom the CB750 proved too big. Faint praise indeed

I decided that the Wheelwrights Motorcycle Club would be my first port of call and, thankfully, a number of members expressed an interest to become instructors. This was of course before the days of DBS certificates, criminal record searches, or background checks at all, so with enough simply saying, '*Yes*' we were in business. Not least as the advertising worked. On Saturday 3rd April 1976 I turned up with my motley group of would-be instructors to meet a full house of spotty trainees. The first session included a basic road safety talk and film. It was conducted by Len Williams and a police officer, but I could tell that the youngsters weren't really interested, so we soon had them all outside where we started with basic machine checks. The trainee's bikes were all basically sound but there were a number of chains that were too loose, too tight or poorly lubricated, so I took the initiative. Getting the spanners out I couldn't help thinking, '*Why didn't someone show me how to do all this when I was still wet behind the ears?*' The idea behind the course was already making sense.

Having arrived under their own steam, the trainees obviously knew how to ride, but you can never presume too much. I demonstrated how to move off safely and smoothly, by finding the biting point of the clutch, with the riders then splitting into threes to practise the same technique with - as I'd guessed - varying degrees of success. We then had them riding around cones, using a stop box and carrying out emergency stops. I was more or less making it up as I went along, but I and all the other instructors were pretty happy all things considered. It looked like we had a course as subsequent weeks saw us on the road, with the Road Safety Officer and police satisfied with the way things had gone: very satisfied as it happened. I was asked if my group of instructors would run further courses. We agreed and it set the pattern for the next few years. From then on we ran about six courses a year and trained hundreds of young riders. It was a lot of fun for us and worthwhile for them. The trainees would all be chatting about what they were being taught, but as young learners there was actually just one question on their minds, *'Who made the fastest 250?'*

'The fastest 250?' One ridden by Charlie Williams of course

Chapter 8
L-Plates, Trailies and Drunks

While legislation later condemned learners to 125cc machines, bikes double their size were allowed up to 1983. The streets teemed with 250s and the first example I had on test was a Yamaha RD250 which, like most of the Yamahas, came from Dugdale's. The 30bhp two-stroke twin was, unsurprisingly, quite similar to the Yamaha 200 that I had owned a few years earlier, though obviously the 250 was somewhat quicker. More noticeable however was the fact that the handling and road-holding had been improved. It was a scaled down 400 after all and the bike was delightfully chuck-able. I was surprised how far Yamaha had come with frame geometry and suspension design in just a few short years, but that I suppose was the purpose of race development. Yamaha twins formed racing's backbone, from club to Grand Prix level, and the RD series were the fruits of that investment. The downside perhaps was that the engine was rather peaky, with maximum torque being achieved high up at 7,000rpm, even if the bike could still burble along at 3,000rpm in an unspectacular fashion. The Yamaha felt what it was: a little racer for the road, with at least one little quirk. In their quest to offer something different the Japanese did throw in a few curve balls: the RD had a stop light warning light. Every time I braked this annoying little dashboard light would become illuminated. Why? It didn't detract from the overall, positive experience however, which was only reinforced shortly afterwards when I tested a Suzuki GT250.

I expected Suzuki's offering to be very similar to the Yamaha. Their earlier 'Super Six' had set the 250 benchmark and the GT was the final evolution of that model. I was in for a surprise however. Rather than finding another little racer, my write-up dubbed the Suzuki a 'Jack of all trades', due to its versatility. The key differences between the Yamaha and the Suzuki were the engine characteristics; both bikes produced similar horsepower, but the Suzuki had more torque at lower revs. Additionally, top gear on the GT operated as an overdrive, dropping the revs at high speed and making motorway work in particular more relaxing. The Yamaha was marginally quicker, but there was little in it until you'd hit illegal speeds. The real difference was in the handling; whilst the Suzuki was perfectly adequate, it didn't have the sharp, race-bred feel of the Yamaha. I would have been happy to tour and ride to work on the Suzuki but the Yamaha was more exciting for a Sunday afternoon blast. Objectively the Yamaha was superior, but Suzuki sold shed-loads of GTs. Who wanted to be Kenny Roberts? Everyone aspired to be Barry Sheene!

If you didn't want to be either there was an answer to that too. The two-stroke brands i.e Suzuki, Kawasaki and Yamaha, were starting to introduce less focussed, four-stroke 250s into their ranges as an alternative. It gave learners an unparalleled choice and when I tested my first 250cc four-stroke roadster my words were, '*Without a doubt, the best of the current crop of 250s that I have ridden.*' These were the concluding words to my test of the Honda CB250T Dream, supplied by Davies Brothers. Looking back, this seems like a strange statement to make about an ugly duckling that only lasted for eighteen months in Honda's range. What led me to that decision? Entirely my own riding preferences. The Dream was extremely comfortable, very smooth - thanks to counter-balancers in the engine - and handled well at legal speeds. It produced 27bhp, which wasn't far short of its competitors but, critically, it was far more relaxing to ride. I suppose what I was really trying to say in my test was that, of all of the current 250s on the UK market, this is the one that I would have bought if I was looking for a long term *keeper*. What I didn't take into account was that most of my readers would have been happier screaming around on an RD250. As the vast majority of 250s were only ever sold as stepping stones, something to pass your test on, before getting a bigger bike at eighteen. No one wheelied a Honda outside the chip shop, you'd never get the front wheel off the ground.

Hondas were *sensible*, not cool and the final 250 that I tested at the time was Yamaha's four-stroke take on that theme, the XS250. This certainly looked more attractive than its Honda rival, having similar styling to the RD range and the same Kenny Roberts speed–block colour scheme. The Yamaha's engine was conventional for a Japanese

I really rated the Honda Dream at the time, though history hasn't treated it so kindly. In retrospect it took bland to a whole new level

lightweight, being a 180° crank four-stroke twin, which unsurprisingly developed identical power to the Honda. As the weight was the same too it wasn't startling to find that the two bikes had very similar performance. Both needed to be revved hard to get the most out of them, but that's where the biggest difference lay: the Honda was smooth, the Yamaha vibrated. It had no fancy balancer mechanism, though they both put one over the two-strokes in having electric starts. The Yamaha probably had the better handling, but customers looking for a sensible learner machine universally bought Hondas. They had a track record of producing 250cc four-stroke twins, and while these got progressively slower and heavier as the years went by, Honda scored a coup the following year when they re-badged the CB250T the Superdream. Stylistically, the Superdream mimicked the recently released CB900F. It had real big bike looks and Honda sold thousands of them. When it came to 250s looks mattered, it was all about image, which also went for two learner legal bikes I *didn't* actually test.

At the time Sondel Sport were selling huge numbers of body kits for RD250s and 400s so Dugdale's got a piece of the action with their own conversions. They were quite popular for a while, helped by Dugdale's racing success

I never got to ride a KH250. As I've mentioned, there were no Kawasaki dealers locally, but it was fairly common knowledge that the *Kwaka* did nothing better than any of the others, apart from have more cylinders. If Mick Grant and Barry Ditchburn were your thing you could even get a lime green body kit – and probably did – as no one could really justify the three-cylinder wheelie machine on any other basis. In truth though, I don't think that there was a bad 250 available in the seventies. They did the job of enabling a generation of young riders to pass their test and do it in some style. As such it was probably just as well that I didn't test an MZ. You see I had a liking for the idiosyncratic East German machines and I went on to own several. I actually preferred them to the more conventional Japanese offerings, as did many others. They sold in their thousands and continued to do so as commuter machines, long after the dreaded 125cc learner law condemned the Japanese machines to history. They were economical, cheap, bullet-proof and, yes, charming, but to have stated that in my column would have branded me as some kind of radical weirdo. There was a get-out clause here though. Having become established I'd receive a lot of press releases directly from the importers, often accompanied by photos. These covered new bikes so I'd include them, space permitting, and take my own photos if images were missing. So, when I look through my photographic archives and see, for example, a CZ175 Trial outside Davies Brothers in Chester, I know it went in the paper, though it was a bike I'd never ridden. Using press release copy avoided me having to make my own judgements. No one would have believed me if I'd said I preferred an MZ or CZ over a Yamaha, but then no one would have believed the following either.

As Steff and I had been married for less than a year, we couldn't afford a week's holiday at the TT in 1976. Of course, because of this it seemed to be continuously discussed in the run-up and I felt totally out of it, until thrown a lifeline. A trip was being organised locally, just for the Senior TT. A plane was being chartered to fly to Ronaldsway, early on the Friday morning and a hotel had even been booked for the Friday night. It sounded like it would be an expensive package so I dismissed it out of hand. However, when I found out the true cost - it was cheap - I instantly said, *'Book me two places. We'll be there!'* Steff was as excited as I was, we couldn't wait.

We turned up at the pub on the Friday morning for the short minibus trip to Liverpool Airport, where we met our pilot who - for reasons that will become apparent – I shan't name. He took us out to a ten-seat Cessna aircraft, which looked a surprisingly small machine. Everyone else's excitement took my mind off any fears however and we took off smoothly and climbed slowly to our cruising height, which wasn't much. At least I could enjoy the view and despite the fact that we hardly seemed to be moving, the flight didn't last very long. The weather on the Island wasn't looking great however. The clouds were down on Snaefell, it was raining hard and before long we heard the dreaded, but not unexpected news we were all awaiting, *'The weather is not expected to improve, racing had been cancelled for the day.'* What were we going to do? Well, there was an impromptu meeting and it was decided that we would get the bus up to Douglas, leave our luggage at the hotel and spend a day in the town amusing ourselves before returning to claim our rooms. On the Saturday, we would hopefully then watch the postponed racing before making our way back to Ronaldsway, to fly home. Thankfully, Saturday dawned much brighter. The racing was declared *on* and over breakfast the pilot confirmed that once the racing had finished and the roads were open, we could all make our way back to the airport. Result!

Steff and I decided to watch from Quarter Bridge as it would be easy to get a bus from there after the racing. It was a good spot anyway and we were hoping to see John Williams do well. The target was the prestigious Classic TT on his Suzuki RG500. Earlier in the week, in the Senior race, John had a good lead over Tom Herron on the final lap but disastrously his bike had stopped at Governor's Bridge, on the run in to the line. John bravely pushed the bike to the flag and then

Eddie Roberts was another of the local stars. At the TT he got a best of fifth in 1976

collapsed with exhaustion. Herron won while John was seventh, with the consolation of taking a new absolute lap record. Everyone knew John should have won and he left no doubters in the Classic as he took the laurels, ahead of Alex George and Tony Rutter, themselves both multiple TT winners. It had been worth coming and as soon as the roads opened, Steff and I caught a bus down to Ronaldsway and sat on a bench and waited…… and waited. Hours passed. I even went as far as looking at where the small aircraft were parked to see if I could recognise ours. Unfortunately, they all looked so similar that I had to admit defeat, wondering, *'Could they have gone without us?'* I was getting really quite agitated, but eventually a taxi turned up and a man stumbled out. Our pilot! We approached and noticed a strong whiff of alcohol: not a good sign I thought, as he asked, *'Where are they?'* When I told him that we were the only ones who'd arrive yet he mumbled some profanity adding, *'Right, let's wait for them ……. in the bar!'* We had little choice but to follow him where we tried, and failed, to encourage him to have non-alcoholic drinks. At one point, he put his arm around Steff and gave her some advice, *'Never say the pilot was drunk; say that he was sociable!'*

Eventually, there was a loud disturbance. The others had arrived, obviously well-oiled themselves and accompanied by a novelty laughing bag, which was frequently and noisily activated, causing great hilarity among the assembled drunks. Additionally, they had acquired an extra passenger. Stan Woods had retired during the Classic race and had scrounged a lift back to Liverpool. He was now probably wishing that he hadn't, as the state of everyone was as clear to him as it was to us, particularly as no one was keen to move on. We might still be there had an airport official not arrived to inform the pilot that he needed to take off in the next few minutes, *'We're shutting for the night, the airport is closing!'* At this our *sociable* pilot cajoled everyone onto the plane and we were soon heading down the runway. We were one passenger heavier than we were when we arrived, no checks seemed to have been carried out and we had an inebriated pilot, but what could I do? In his defence the take-off was perfect, though once en route the pilot did appear to close his eyes and fall asleep. The aircraft stayed straight and level however – the wonders of auto-pilot I imagine – we landed without problem and the pilot staggered from the Cessna, I presume for an early night. I felt like kissing the ground, but resisted the temptation finding it hard to believe what had just happened. Next time we'd be sailing.

The rest of 1976 seemed to pass rather uneventfully when compared to the Isle of Man trip and it wasn't really until the following year that I had any truly interesting bikes to test. They were, on reflection, an eclectic mix and the first on the scene was Yamaha's brand new XS750. This certainly bucked recent trends by having three cylinders rather than four and a shaft-drive instead of a chain. Coming late to the big four-stroke market, Yamaha clearly wanted to do things differently while adding a touch of class and respectability. *'Super Shaft'* ran the adverts, featuring a female black model, clearly trying to tap in to the vibe of the cool American Shaft detective series which was popular at the time. The double-overhead-camshaft engine was certainly sophisticated, but also proved to be something of a wolf in sheep's clothing.

It was a pussycat, happy to trundle along at low revs in a high gear, but then quickly transformed into a tiger once the throttle was fully wound on. It could certainly pick its feet up in a satisfying fashion. In my test, I remarked that the Yamaha had a European feel to it, similar to its XS650 stable-mate and this wasn't an illusion. I didn't know it at the time but Norton had been using one on test, ostensibly to assess its potential as a police Interpol replacement, but mainly to sort the handling. They were also employed by Yamaha to build their HL500 off-road competition bike and there was certainly European DNA in the XS750. It reminded me of a BMW rather, with similar engine characteristics and, of course, that low-maintenance shaft final-drive. The XS750 carried its weight well, handled and, looking back, of all the Japanese Superbikes I ever rode, the XS750 was my favourite. I admired Yamaha for daring to be different and for once so did the voting public. It was MCN *Machine of the Year* in 1977, but *voting* didn't mean *buying*. Yamaha's gamble was not rewarded at the till. Bike buyers wanted nothing less than four cylinders, though as an aside my colleague Bob Edwards was sufficiently impressed to buy one after his Honda 400/4. There was also an amusing outcome of my write-up.

The appearance of my XS750 road test in the paper led to an irate phone call from an incandescent Alan Dugdale. When, as was my habit, I had taken copies of the paper to his shop on the Friday morning, Alan had been out. So, I left them in his office as it was he who had lent me the bike. Back at the Observer a few hours later, I had a very unhappy Alan screaming at me down the phone, *'Are you trying to make me a laughing stock?'* he ranted.

As Alan was making no sense at all, I said that I would come and see him straight away and this calmed him down. Before I left however I re-read my article and I could not find anything within it that could possibly have caused the row. It was very perplexing, but by the time I got to Dugdale's Alan was still not a happy bunny. I managed to stay calm as I asked what the problem was and, *'There!'* he shouted, stabbing his finger at my photograph of the bike. The picture had been taken in Dugdale's car park and I could see nothing wrong with it. My puzzled look only served to infuriate Alan further, *'There, look!'* he fumed as his finger prodded at a particular part of the photograph. I had a closer look - and I *really* did have to look – and on closer inspection, in the very far distance, I could see some washing, drying on a neighbour's line. I tried not to laugh as I explained to Alan with as straight a face as possible that the washing wasn't going to affect sales, but he wasn't to be placated. He muttered threats about never providing test bikes again and never advertising with the Observer so all I could do was to leave him and his rage, apologising again as I made an uncomfortable exit.

I wasn't in the least surprised when, a week later, Alan rang up to offer me another test bike, as if nothing had ever happened. I wasn't going to mention it as - without being arrogant - I knew by now that Alan needed me, more than I needed him. I was providing free publicity and shops like Dugdale's needed it. There were plenty to choose from and the manufacturers largely let the technology do the talking. It was hard to move stock when the manufacturers were constantly innovating and introducing new models, so publicity for any older models was priceless, Honda's 750 four being a case in point. The CB750 had changed the face of motorcycling. The name Honda was on everyone's lips at the start of the decade, as unlike the British, the Japanese didn't sit back on their laurels. For a while however the CB750 languished, as Honda raised the technological bar again when they introduced the Gold Wing only a few years later.

The Gold Wing was designed by a project team headed by Shoichiro Irimajiri, the man who had worked on Honda's amazing Grand Prix bike engines in the 1960s and the new engine was certainly innovative. It was the first Japanese four-stroke to feature a water-cooled engine and what an engine: a 999cc single-overhead-camshaft flat-four, coupled to a shaft final-drive. With 'boxer' engines like this the torque reaction always causes a rocking motion, particularly at slow speed, but Honda cleverly counteracted this by having a generator that rotated in the opposite direction to the crank. It was an idea they took one step further with the CX500, having the clutch and gearbox rotating in the opposite direction instead.

That was later though. The GL1000 was introduced in October 1974 and it was a well-established model by the time that I got to test one in 1977. I'd ridden plenty of big bikes by now, so while the sheer size of the *Wing* remained intimidating, the way that the Honda carried its bulk low down made it quite easy to ride. It was smooth, it was quiet and it was a top gear bike that made gear changing an optional extra. At most speeds I would get it into top as soon as was practical and just stay there. At 70mph the engine was only turning at 3,000rpm. It made for very relaxed riding as it disguised its 602lb weight well. The Gold Wing was not designed for chucking about however. It was sure-footed certainly, just as long as sudden changes of direction weren't attempted. The bike was made for distance work and a one-day, two-up, ride to and from the Croft race circuit in North Yorkshire proved that this was the Honda's forte. Even the climb up the Trans-Pennine M62 motorway was handled in effortless style. Though having said that, there was a price to pay; on that trip the GL1000 only returned 35mpg. This was a bike for the tourer, but only if they had deep pockets. That was doubly frustrating as, while the Gold Wing was an ideal distance bike, it had an oddly small fuel tank which necessitated overly frequent stops. In the States the Gold Wing was a huge success;

Honda even built a factory there. But, technological marvel that it was, many British riders dismissed it as a two-wheeled car. In truth we had neither the roads nor distances to accommodate it. British riders had been happier with Honda's original, seminal, across the frame four, so when Tom Loughridge loaned me the latest model, the Honda CB750F2, or *Super Sport*, I was keen to see if it still had the same aura. The basic model was now seven or eight years old.

The original CB750 had been followed by numerous 'K' models, one to eight I think, but the styling of the last model, the F1, had been universally slated. It attempted to mimic the hugely successful 400/4, with four, curvy down-pipes and pseudo-café racer styling, but failed. As such Honda had redesigned the bike with a black engine, an upswept silencer and Comstar wheels, which were Honda's take on the move away from wire-spoked wheels. The engine now had bigger valves too, as well as a different camshaft to enable higher revs, since Suzuki and Kawasaki in particular had shown what riders had come to expect i.e. more power and higher top speeds: no one production raced a K-Series CB750. The new bike was solid, smooth and quite fast but, despite the updates, it seemed to be showing its age. As I've said previously, I didn't ride a contemporary Kawasaki Z1 until sometime later, but when I did I realised that it would have eaten the Honda for breakfast. The 750 handled OK, but it wasn't balanced in the way that say a Laverda, Ducati or a BMW was: the original Honda CB750 was nearing the end of the road.

If I had been pressed to choose which of the last three Superbikes I'd have wanted, as I said, it would have been the Yamaha. But of all of the Superbikes that I'd *ever* tested, none of my favourites were actually Japanese. My choices would have been the BMW 900s - the R90/6 and R90S - the Ducati GT750 and the Laverda twin: the BMW R90/6 for everyday practicality and serious touring, the R90S for fast mile-munching, the Ducati for glorious handling and a great soundtrack and the Laverda for its rock-solid predictability. Incidentally, I had the chance to ride an R90/6 again in 2021 and I was reminded of what a great motorbike it still is. I had custody of a Ducati GT750 too, a few years after my road test, and that longer acquaintance with the bike only reinforced my original very high opinion of its abilities. Machines like the Ducati 750 were of course largely fantasy bikes however. Most riders had smaller, more affordable machines and the biggest sellers were learner legal 250s. I'd said previously, that every rider wanted the fastest 250 out there and that the Japanese offered a wide range of two and four-stroke twins, Kawasaki even having a 250cc triple. However, that wasn't the full story. You didn't have to have a full 250, nor a multi. There was a whole different market out there for simpler, bare-bones machines and I knew all about it. When it came to testing trail bikes, I had an advantage. By now I was a pretty experienced green lane rider, so I could genuinely analyse the off-road ability of this type of machine. There was no impostor syndrome on my part, I knew what to look for and the usual question begging to be asked, *'Did the manufacturer really intend this trail bike to be used off-road?'* The vast majority of trail bikes were only ever ridden on the road; a bit like the Adventure bikes of today. Riders bought them because they looked good and had style. As my time with my little Yamaha DT125 had shown, if they really were to be used off-road, virtually all trail bikes needed modification. So how did my little selection of standard machines, straight out of the crate, perform when I took them green laning?

The first bike that I tested was Honda's XL250 Motosport. The 20bhp, 250cc overhead-camshaft engine featured four valves per cylinder and was carried in a purposeful and compact package. I asked in advance if I could take it off-road, as there was every chance it would get bumped and scraped if used as god intended and was pleased when the dealer said they were more than happy. The engine pulled like a little tractor, the bike being unfazed by mud or steep climbs and, despite being heavier than its two-stroke rivals, the Honda coped really well with all but the tightest of trails. I was impressed, really impressed in fact. With a few sensible modifications weight could be shed from an already light machine to make it even more capable: Mr Honda got ten out of ten for this one.

Prior to the 400/4 and XS750 Bob Edwards had a Yamaha DT175, so this was an easy one to test. He actually offered it without me asking, and I was really interested as it was effectively a larger version of my own off-road machine. I had only ridden it a few yards before I realised that it was, unsurprisingly very similar, just with more mid-range performance and torque, and as a result I didn't take it on a proper green lane. I rode it to the start of a track on Moel Arthur, near Mold, as this was close enough in terms of getting some authentic looking photographs. At the time I was more interested in another Yamaha. This was a DT250, which I had on loan from Davies Brothers. Yamaha can lay claim to inventing the modern trail bike with their original 250 DT1 and this bike was a direct descendant. While the 175 was just a grown up 125 I immediately noticed that the DT250 was a little bigger. It retained the same riding position however which was comfortable, both sitting or standing, and the single-cylinder two-stroke engine certainly had plenty of go. It had been wisely tuned for low and mid-range grunt however, even if Yamaha knew more were probably ridden on tarmac than dirt. It was actually a bit of a compromise, but very well done. The whole package made for a sprightly road bike, with good acceleration and easy handling, though once off road the DT was still an excellent proposition for green laning. It coped well with both muddy and rocky climbs and hid its weight well, even if it didn't quite have the balance of its smaller siblings. I preferred a friend's 250 Ossa Explorer off-road, but the Yamaha was a much better bike on tarmac. Few people could afford the luxury of a bike purely for off road riding, so Yamaha probably shifted a hundred DT250s for every Ossa sold.

My final trail bike test was a big one: Yamaha's XT500, this one from Dugdale's. When I collected it, Alan asked if I would be able to start it. I thought he was joking. I had read that *'the drill'* had to be followed and, with judicious use of the valve-lifter and a traditional long swinging kick, it started. I wondered, *'What was he on about?'* I soon found out. Unfortunately, the XT flattered to deceive. Things weren't the same when the engine was hot: starting became very hit and miss. Once going though, the engine was delightful, having bags of low-down grunt and really strong acceleration. On the road, it was a very pleasant bike to ride, having a good balance of power and handling. On the green lanes however, it was a different proposition; it was

Trying the XT500 off road. In truth it was more suited to tarmac…. if you could start it

simply too heavy for anything but the easiest going. Admittedly, a big, strong, rider would have loved it, but I simply didn't have the muscle to haul it around. The XT500 *looked* like an off-roader but ninety-five percent of them spent all of their time on the road. That wasn't a criticism as it made for a very good road bike, once you'd got it started! Given that I'd got a Yamaha myself and tested three more, of all the trail bikes that I rode, the Honda XL250 actually had the greatest potential. It had a lovely, forgiving motor and was commendably light. Improved gearing would have made it a serious, potentially great trail bike and my write-up said as much. Incidentally, should anyone be wondering, *'Why all this about trail bikes?'* they were and still are *hugely* popular in the North West, no, the north in general, simply as we have the terrain. You wouldn't sell many in Essex, but around the Pennines and in North Wales there was a big market and both myself and the Observer sales team were aware of that.

Chapter 9
Barry Sheene, Fizzies and Chairs

B ack on the track, as the 1976 season came to a close, Allen Steele realised that he would have to change engines again. That was just to remain competitive, forgetting becoming more so. Although big two-strokes were starting to dominate the domestic sidecar scene, they were massively expensive, so Allen decided to go a more cost-effective route and buy a four-cylinder Kawasaki 1000 motor from Bill Smith. With no sign of sponsorship on the horizon, friends put their hands in their pockets to help out and Steff and I managed to scrape together £40. It was earmarked for some pistons so I took the money over to Allen's one dinnertime, where I expected him to be delighted. He was, but not in the way I'd expected, *'Thanks for the money John, but I'll use it for something else if that's alright, we don't need pistons anymore.'* My obviously bewildered look led to an excited explanation, Allen hitting me with the short version first, *'We've got an ex-works Suzuki engine, and some sponsorship!'* He'd been approached by ex-Suzuki GB race technician Bob White who was the mechanic for John Williams. Bob had left Suzuki, but with backing from Bill Smith he was setting up a Suzuki dealership in Chester. Suzuki GB knew of Bob's plans and were very supportive so allowed him to have an ex-works 750 triple engine plus loads of spares. The idea was for him to get involved in sidecar racing.

To have an engine identical to those used recently by Barry Sheene, John Williams and Tepi Länsivuori was an incredible boost to Allen's chances in 1977. The existing sidecar chassis was modified to suit the new engine and everything was ready for an exciting season: or so we thought. The outfit had shown great promise at a short Oulton Park test session, but at the first meeting of the season the engine seized in practice. Allen rebuilt it with new pistons but it seized again in the race. This pattern was repeated at a number of meetings, despite the fact that Allen and Bob White had gone through it with a fine tooth-comb; they'd changed everything they could think of, in some cases several times. At Croft, I had travelled up on the Honda Gold Wing I was testing, with Steff on the back, and we arrived just in time to see Allen and Tony touring back to the pits during practice, with yet another seizure. The engine was rapidly stripped and with no spare pistons left, Allen and Bob dejectedly cleaned up the ones they'd used in practice. Everyone was at a loss to understand the cause of the seizures, so Tony suggested that, as everything else had been tried, it could be worth taking off the Amal carburettors and fitting the spare, original, Mikunis. With nothing to lose, they did it. None of us had very high expectations for a finish, and Allen had already decided to go steadily, to see how far he got before seizing again. When, at about half distance all was well, he pulled his finger out and managed to climb as high as fourth. We were all delighted, but we were even happier when Allen and Tony won the second race. Everyone was relieved, but also a bit mystified.

Allen would never admit to it, but he was and still is a great analytical thinker. I knew that he would have been running over the problem in his head, to such an extent that I was sure he'd have an explanation by the time I next called round: he had. The Amal carburettors had been fitted on the advice of John Williams. He had told Bob that TR750 engines were faster when fitted with Amals than with the standard Mikunis. Allen had worked out that whilst this was the case with a solo, it caused problems in an outfit. The forces acting on a sidecar are very different to those on a solo. These caused fuel starvation, called 'swill', when cornering on an outfit. This was due to how the fuel was picked up in the float bowls and it was different in the Mikunis to the Amals. That was it then, problem solved. After Allen and Tony had switched to the Mikunis they had a successful first half of the season, with many leaderboard placings against top-level opposition. Whilst not as fast as the four-cylinder TZ700 Yamaha engines which were proliferating, the Suzuki developed good torque and, from that point onwards, was very reliable. Suddenly it was full steam ahead and everything went up a gear. Allen sent off an entry for the TT and we all started planning accordingly.

You've probably noticed that I tested a disproportionate number of larger, prestige, machines. It was true, but purely by chance. I didn't

The new Suzuki TR750 powered outfit. It was highly successful after early teething problems, though it never quite had the legs of a Yamaha TZ 700/750

seem to get many sub-250cc class bikes, probably as dealers thought, *'Oh, he'll not be interested in the latest 125 commuter.'* I should have been, and was, as that was what my readership were probably buying. They did come along however, and my first small test bike was Honda's CB200 four-stroke twin. At the time, the 200cc class was popular, mainly as a 200 was considerably cheaper to insure than a 250. It was interesting to compare the latest Honda 200 to its CB175 predecessor, as the 175 had been my brother's first proper motorcycle and my first thought was, *'What have they done to the styling?'* The CB175 was good-looking, in an old-school, conservative sort of way and Honda to my mind had taken a seriously wrong turn with the update.

The CB200's slab-sided fuel tank looked awful. Everyone remembers the green ones, with their weird, quilted top, petrol tank, even if the rest of the bike was fundamentally sound. Riding the CB200, everything was very familiar: easy controls, smooth, revvy engine and, apart from bouncy rear shock absorbers, good handling. The 17bhp engine was a typical little Honda, it cried out to be ridden hard and it came back for more. The bike was a great little commuter and fun to ride at the same time, so I could have forgiven any other shortcoming it might have had if it wasn't for its very odd looks. I dubbed it, *'The perfect all rounder'* as it was, if you could forget the aesthetics. Of a similar capacity, Dugdale's provided me with a Yamaha RD200, which again was going back to familiar territory. Compared to the YCS3 that I had owned, the new 200 looked far sportier, with Yamaha's corporate speed-block design on the fuel tank and side panels. The engine produced an identical amount of power to my YCS3 (22bhp) so, as expected, performance was similar too. If plenty of use was made of the upper reaches of the power band, it really punched above its weight. There was of course a price to be paid in fuel consumption, but little two-strokes weren't really bought to tootle around on. The handling was great in all conditions and it was easy to take liberties with the little Yam. In the 200 class, Honda won on practicality, Yamaha on having fun.

The distinction of being the smallest capacity bike that I ever tested fell to Yamaha's FS1E DX *'Sports Moped'*. These bikes existed due to the law which allowed sixteen-year-olds to ride mopeds. To make the most of this legislation, manufacturers fitted pedals to 50cc motorbikes so that they technically met the criteria. By the following year, the law required such bikes to be restricted to 30mph, but the bike I tested was the last of the unrestricted machines and the *'Fizzie'* was enormous fun: good looking, great handling, ridiculously light weight, capable of around 45mph and it even had a front disc brake. No wonder sixteen-year-olds lusted after them and bought them and crashed them in equal quantities; it's probably why they are so valuable today. If I'd been sixteen again I'd have had one like a shot, though I don't think that's exactly how I put it in my test. Parents would be reading – and paying – so I had to be circumspect.

In truth my only other small bike test covered one of the unsung heroes of the motorcycling world, the Honda CG125. I have to confess that this little bike is a favourite of mine and over the years I have owned several. The CG is a basic 125cc four-stroke single with pushrod-operated valves and a fully enclosed chain. Commuters who wanted a conventional motorcycle rather than a Honda *Step-thru* bought them in their droves due to their ruggedness, reliability and fantastic fuel economy. The CG was designed with a pushrod engine as, without regular maintenance and oil changes, Honda's alternative, the overhead-cam CB125, would suffer camshaft damage. The original idea was for the CG to be sold primarily in developing countries, but their virtues were not lost on British buyers. Of course, the 10.8bhp engine was hardly fast, but even when ridden flat out everywhere it would achieve well over 100mpg. I still think that the CG125 makes common sense for commuting on our crowded urban roads and I'm obviously not the only one. As I write, Chinese CG copies can still be bought and the British Historic Racing Club even has a category for just this sort of bike. You don't change something if it ain't broken, you just update it.

Another machine which fitted the keeping-an-old-idea-modern theme came up soon after the CG125 test. I was used to receiving cryptic phone calls from Alan Dugdale, so when he asked me one day if I could come to collect a surprise machine it certainly piqued my interest. Despite his foibles, Alan wouldn't waste my time, so a couple of days later, I presented myself at his Alvanley showrooms to find out that I was about to borrow……. a sidecar outfit. A smiling Alan explained that he thought Yamaha's XS650 engine would be ideal for an outfit, for which Squire Sidecars had supplied him with an ST1 as the model they thought best suited.

The handsome result of Alan's efforts was sitting around the back of the showrooms waiting for me and certainly looked the part, with the white sidecar in contrast to the black motorcycle. I tried to explain that, whilst I understood the *theory* of sidecarring, I'd never actually driven one, but undeterred, Alan told me that I would soon get the hang of it, leaving me with the ambiguous comment, '*Remember, your right hand is your best friend.*' As the outfit had stickers pronouncing, '*H. Dugdale Motors Demonstrator*' he wanted me to keep it a couple of weeks and, in his words, '*Put it about a bit*'. He wanted the thing sold. '*At least I'm familiar with the bike*' I thought. When I'd road tested Tom Loughridge's XS650, I had got on with it really well. So, I only had the third wheel to get used to: *only!* Once on the outfit, I completed a few laps of the car park without any problem. But I was only doing about 10mph and riding down the steep lane, from Dugdale's to the main Frodsham-Chester road, I realised that I would have to negotiate a few tight bends and that was a bit unnerving. The theory was that the driver of an outfit should accelerate around left-hand bends, making the bike go around the sidecar. Conversely you were meant to brake on right-handers, to get the sidecar to come around the bike.

That was the principle, but of course the first bend I came to – force of habit - I tried to lean. I got down the hill though, safely if very slowly and once on the main road I picked up a bit of speed. Despite having to consciously concentrate on the technique, to avoid slipping back to solo mode, I began to enjoy myself. I became more confident and I found that I could actually travel reasonably quickly. It was fun and reasonably practical, while Steff and other passengers who tried the sidecar said that it was comfortable too, if a little noisy. I took the outfit to the Wheelwrights Club and to the weekly training course session and it created lots of interest, though whether anyone forked out the £1,275 that Dugdale's were asking, I never actually knew.

You might also ask why Dugdale's were trying to market such an arcane device anyway, but in the 1970s there was still a hardcore market. You'd always see outfits at rallies and with leading-link forks – which Alan's combination didn't actually have - and much better sidecars, outfits had never been better. To my surprise I discovered that I really enjoyed the Yamaha and some years later I owned an MZ outfit which I loved, especially in the snow. I don't think I've ever got the experience out of my system to be honest, and having learned how to pilot one, it only increased my admiration for those who raced them, as Allen and Tony did.

I'd left them sending off their entry for the 1977 TT and of course Steff and I were making plans to go too. That was until we had our legs pulled out from under us. On one of my regular visits to see Allen, I could tell that something was wrong before he had even spoken, Allen's face was livid, *'You won't believe this'* he said through gritted

The XS650 outfit. It was an acquired taste which… I clearly acquired. Riding it made me fully appreciate the skill of racers such as Allen

teeth, *'The ***** ing bastards have refused my entry!'* Of course, I asked the obvious question and Allen stuttered, *'Why? Because I haven't got enough experience!!!!!'* I was about to say, *'But you won the Manx Grand Prix'* until I realised that this wouldn't help.

Allen was crestfallen, angry and speechless, which for him must have been a first. I didn't hang around, as Allen in a bad mood was a frightening thing to behold. I just went home to Steff, to break the bad news that we wouldn't be going to that year's races. When I dared to call at Allen's sometime the following week, he was back to his normal cheery self; in fact he was unusually happy. *'Great news'* he said *'We're going to the Island!'* So I sat down with the inevitable mug of tea to hear the tale that had brought about Allen's transformation. Bob White had suggested he try for an entry in the Southern 100, another race on the Isle of Man. I knew very little about it but Allen explained that it was held in July, on four and a quarter miles of road around Castletown, known as the Billown circuit. When Allen had contacted the race organiser they had immediately replied, *'Not the Allen Steele who won the Manx?'* After which it had all been plain sailing. As we were short of cash I decided I'd go over just for the Sidecar Championship race, knowing full well that this was a gamble. I'd have to fly again, so had to hope against the previous appalling weather, drunk pilots, and Allen and Tony failing to qualify, as there were heats before the final. Come the day however it looked like our plans were scuppered from a different angle. As I was walking down the main road to Castletown from the airport, I recognised a familiar van coming the other way. Allen saw me waving, pulled up and opened the driver's window, *'Jump in John, we're just going up to Nobles Hospital to see Adjers.'* My heart sank. Allen and Tony – *Adjers* as he was known - obviously wouldn't be competing. I was surprised therefore that Allen seemed quite upbeat about the situation and, on the drive to Douglas, all became clear, although it still sounds improbable.

Allen and Tony had been leading the qualifying race. All had been going to plan when, late in proceedings, Tony had hit Allen on the back. Taking this as a, *'Someone's catching us'* signal, Allen put the hammer down and pressed on. However, a couple of corners later, the sidecar came up in the air and Allen turned to see Tony lying unconscious on the platform floor! As it was the last lap and he was still leading, Allen held Tony in place with his left hand. Crossing the finish line and having won, Allen then rode directly across to where the St. John's Ambulance crews were standing, shouting, *'I think I've hit my mate's head on a wall.'* Slowly, Tony regained consciousness and was able to tell everyone gathered round that it wasn't his head that was the problem: the cartilage in his knee had actually become displaced. Tony had been hitting Allen to get him to stop, so that he could push the cartilage back into place, as he'd been able to do previously, when the same thing had happened playing football. When Allen hadn't stopped, Tony had passed out from the excruciating pain. In no time at all, a physiotherapist was located and Tony's knee was attended to. But what of the all-important question, *'Is he fit to race?'* The physio thought that as long as he rested the leg, there wouldn't be a problem. Great, except we hadn't factored in Tony being Tony. He ignored the advice and that evening, as part of his *rest and recuperation* whilst dancing in a Douglas nightspot, there was an almighty, audible, 'crack' which announced that: a) hospitalisation would be required, and b) Tony wouldn't be racing!

Sidecar racers are a tough breed however and Allen hadn't given up. He heard that a fellow competitor, Bill Hall, had blown his Kawasaki engine up and now wouldn't be racing. So, Allen approached his passenger, Pete Minion, to ask if he was available. He was, so the pair went off to Race Control, to organise the change of passenger. When asked the inevitable, 'Have you raced together before?' question, both lied convincingly and the change was duly authorised. The paddock was the first time I'd met Pete and he seemed very laid back for someone who was about to get onto an unfamiliar outfit, with a new driver, having done no practice to race between dry stone walls and pillar boxes. Sidecar passengers are a different breed.

The pair of them were making it up as they went along, but they got away to a good start and were with the leading group as they disappeared from sight, rounding the right hander at Ballakeighan. As the leaders appeared at Castletown Corner at the end of the lap, Allen was still there, challenging near the front and before too long, the crackling radio commentary announced, 'Allen Steele and Pete Minion are in the lead.' I was praying for the race to end, but Allen actually kept increasing his advantage, the outfit sounding fantastic, right up to the point that they ducked under the chequered flag. If we'd had any champagne we would have opened it. They'd won and Allen's first words after taking his helmet off were, 'Now let them try to refuse my *****ing TT entry next year!'

1977 had been a pretty good year, in 1978 I had a lot to look forward to. I was still writing my weekly column, road test machines were being spontaneously offered on a fairly regular basis, green lane riding was still an enjoyable and important part of my life, and Allen Steele and Tony Barrow's prospects for the following sidecar racing season were looking good. I was also still heavily involved in the motorcycle training scheme, alongside a terrific group of fellow instructors with whom I had become great friends. OK, the advertising part of my job at the Cheshire Observer was still just a means to an end, but I could hardly complain. I think the same could be said for Allen as while he would have happily continued with his current Suzuki TR750 engine, for at least another season, sponsor Bob White helpfully intervened. He had his sights set on higher targets than the ageing three-cylinder Suzuki engine could achieve. He wanted the Bob White Racing Team – for that's what it now was - to be properly competitive in the British Championship: he had other plans. The team would have a new outfit for 1978 and what a combo it would be. He bought the sidecar which had just won the 1977 British Sidecar Championship and had finished tenth in the World Championship: it was the Windle TZ700 of Bill Hodgkins and John Parkin.

It was widely acknowledged that Terry Windle constructed some of the best outfits around. Terry designed and hand-built these works of art in his workshop, at Thurgoland in West Yorkshire, and the outfits were not just good to look at. They won five World Championships over the years and I first saw this one at a shakedown session over the winter. It was still painted in the battle-worn colours of Bill Hodgkins' sponsor, the legendary Joe Francis, but it still looked really purposeful whichever way you looked at it. Allen and Tony took to it immediately and over the winter it was checked over with a fine toothcomb, repainted, and once finished looked absolutely beautiful. The design was based on Yamaha's original, iconic, American speed-block pattern as first used by the likes of Kenny Roberts, however the base colour of the outfit was black instead of yellow, with red blocks over white. The whole effect was stunning and many people, myself included, thought it was the best looking outfit around. Barry Sheene certainly thought so, he copied the design on his 1980 Akai Yamahas: we should have taken out a patent.

There were a few problems in the early part of the season, but there were also some good results, including at Aintree, where Allen won. That was a good omen for the TT, for which an entry had been sent off and accepted, even if Allen wasn't exactly happy. After his refusal the year previously Allen had now been given a start number of 74. This bore no relation to his National ranking nor ability and meant he would be starting behind seventy-three other outfits. The possibility of getting any sort of result whilst trying to pass that many slower machines was highly unlikely and Bob White thought that Allen's start number wasn't coincidental. Bob had previously been involved in an argument with the ACU official who allocated the numbers and he was sure that this chap was getting his own back. Nevertheless, an entry was an entry and we all made plans.

The TT would be momentous, unforgettable actually, but before that there was one other, particularly interesting, race meeting that I would have to attend. The Anglo-American Transatlantic races took place every Easter and a week or so before the 1978 series began I received a request from Bob. The Brands Hatch races were on Good Friday, the Mallory Park round on the Saturday and our own local Oulton Park races on the Bank Holiday Monday, March 27th. Bob asked me if I could ride a new bike to Oulton Park for him and while I guessed that this would be used in some kind of publicity stunt, to promote his newly opened Suzuki Centre, he told me he'd fill in the details when I picked it up. When I did, I found out that there was more to the arrangement than I'd thought: I wasn't just the delivery man. The bike was a brand new GS1000 and the deal was that I would take the big Suzuki to the circuit and then, at the appointed time, ride it to the start/finish line, where Barry Sheene would take over. Barry would then ride it round for a lap in front of what would be tens of thousands of fans. As those old enough will remember, the Transatlantic races were hugely popular, you couldn't hope for bigger crowds.

The reason for the GS1000 was that it was Suzuki's brand new, flagship model. I got a few freebies, like press passes to the Racing & Sporting Motorcycle Show each year, but these perks didn't extend to Paris Motorcycle Show tickets, where the big GS had been glimpsed by a lucky few, in prototype form only, the previous Autumn. I don't think anyone realised quite how near that mock-up was to production however. It was very near, as earlier in March one hundred and forty GS1000s had arrived, quietly, into the UK, largely undetected. Each major Suzuki dealership was allocated just one bike and there was quite a buzz growing around them. Just days earlier Steve McLaughlin had taken a GS1000 to its first victory at the Daytona 200 races in the

USA and everyone was clamouring to see one. I'd certainly never clapped eyes on one before and neither had anyone else in this country; its arrival at Oulton Park was going to make a huge splash.

I picked up the bike from Bob's showroom the night before the races and found, as I'd expected, that even running-in it felt a hugely sophisticated, powerful bit of kit. It was quoted as producing anywhere between 83bhp and 90bhp - depending on the imagination of whoever was writing - and I was acutely aware of the figures as I rode this pristine example home. It had been polished to within an inch of its life and we couldn't afford any mishaps; God forbid that I might drop it. Luckily, when I got out of bed on Monday it was a fine, bright,

Left to right, Bob White, Barry Sheene, Eric Pope (Chief Scrutineer) and myself. The caption to the photo in the Observer actually said, *'and right, Racing Correspondent John Moulton.'* Odd, I thought I was being paid as an advertising salesman?

morning on which to ride the big Suzuki to the circuit. It received plenty of admiring glances as I parked it in the paddock next to Bob White's Transit van where I hung around fending off the obvious questions. Then, as the grid was being assembled for the first Match Race, I got the thumbs up, the signal to ride it round. I very self-consciously trundled it onto the circuit, past all the priceless racing machinery to the very front of what was a stellar, Grand Prix-quality grid. I'd never ridden in front of so many people before, nor been in such exalted company. I didn't have time to be star-struck though, as Bob introduced me to Barry cameras snapped away and Barry, being Barry, he then went totally off-script.

Never one to do things by half-measures, Barry managed to persuade American riders Dave Aldana and Skip Aksland to get on the bike with him and the *three* of them then completed a lap, waving enthusiastically to the ecstatic crowd. I don't know what Yamaha thought – Aldana and Aksland were riding TZ750s – but Suzuki got some good free publicity and on the bike's return, Barry handed it back to me, saying to Bob, *'Don't worry, I didn't take it over 4,000 revs.'* As Skip Aksland was sitting on his lap I very much doubt he could see any of the instruments, but who was to doubt Barry Sheene? As the cheers for Barry and his friends subsided and under the watchful eyes of tens of thousands, I then rode the bike back to the paddock, to slightly less applause. It was actually pretty stressful, though there was an interesting postscript to the ride.

I parked-up the GS and watched the racing like everybody else for the rest of the day. I came back however to find a chap in leathers and a green Castrol paddock jacket looking at the big Suzuki. He must have recognised me as the rider parading the bike earlier as he asked me what I thought of it. I could see that he was genuinely interested as he continued to ask astute questions, even if I sometimes struggled to understand his heavy Scottish accent. We chatted away and after a while I saw that his name was embroidered on the front of his jacket: *Jock Taylor*. I guess I might have heard his name before, but little did I know that the quiet enthusiast I was casually chatting to was a World Champion in the making. It had been a long day and by the end I was just relieved to be able to return the Suzuki to Bob's showroom unmolested; a great responsibility had been lifted from my shoulders. It was worth it though, just to chat to Jock Taylor and Barry Sheene; it was surprising what you might get up to, working on a local newspaper. It made for quite a day, but an even more momentous one was just around the corner.

One of my better photos of Barry at Oulton Park. I was rather pleased with the way I caught his helmet, though I don't think this one ever made it into Motorcycle Scene

Chapter 10
A Job in the Trade

Soon after, in Tom Loughridge's showroom, he asked me if I could put an advert in the Observer, for an extra member of staff. After he had dictated the copy, Tom seemed a bit hesitant, which was unusual for him. He glanced across the office at his wife and then, turning back to me almost sheepishly enquired, *'Unless, of course, you'd like to come and work here for us?'* I was stunned, but Tom explained that he and his wife Ann had been wondering if I would be interested in working in the trade as he had a bit of a plan. He wanted to expand the business, by opening another branch and, if I was interested and once trained, I could eventually take that new branch on. He pointed out that the money wouldn't be great, but I was hooked the minute he'd opened his mouth. I said that I would ask Steff what she thought of the idea but in my head the answer was already, *'Yes'.*

Steff was totally supportive. She knew that I'd be happier working for Tom and I immediately handed in my notice at the paper. I would never forget the opportunities given to me by the Cheshire Observer and this still might sound like an odd decision. Instead of riding Superbikes I'd be fixing them, but the truth was that I was an advertising salesman ninety-five percent of the time and my column was totally un-funded. Writing could never have become a full-time proposition at the Observer and I hated the advertising side of things. It was time to move on, so I did, on a Honda 125.

Money was tight and I genuinely liked the little Honda, even if it was a bit underpowered for the daily commute. It was thirty-four miles to Tom's and back and I admit to being surprisingly apprehensive on my first ride over; I didn't know what to expect. Tom calmed me down immediately though, by welcoming me with a storeman's coat and by getting me to scrape old stickers off the showroom's windows. I didn't mind at all, I loved the simplicity of a manual task after years behind a desk. Besides which, over the following weeks and months, I spent time in the stores, in the workshop and on the sales floor, experiencing the peculiarities of every aspect. I also collected bikes in the shop van from our storage depot - a grand name for some space on a chicken farm - as well as delivering customer bikes. I was lucky in having a good working knowledge of current models, but I still had challenges, particularly as I had a condition to work around. I particularly enjoyed building new bikes up, straight from the crate, though I struggled with the wiring: I'm colour-blind.

It didn't matter, I loved every minute of it and I'm taken back to my time driving Tom's ex-police V6 Ford Transit to '*The Ranch*' - as our storage depot had been christened - whenever I hear a Neil Diamond song. The van had an eight-track tape machine and Tom's only tape for it, you guessed it, was Neil Diamond's Greatest Hits. It became the soundtrack to my wonderful early working life at Tom's which, from May onwards, saw Tom's thoughts preoccupied with preparations for that year's Isle of Man TT. He was due to ride his Crooks T500 Suzuki again, in the Production race, and a TZ250 Maxton Yamaha in the Junior. In addition, our workshop housed Charlie Williams' 250 and 350 Maxton Yamahas. Tom had sponsored Charlie in 1977, when he had won the Junior race, and he would do so again in 1978. As a result the shop had a fine selection of race machinery on show prior to the biggest event of the year. I'd be part of that, but I realised I'd become part of the wider racing scene already.

Even though Bob White was now running his own business, he was still heavily involved in racing. As sponsor and mechanic, he was at every meeting with Allen and it soon became obvious that he knew *everyone* in the paddock. He had fingers in many pies. At one International at Cadwell Park, he stepped in to help his rider from Suzuki GB days, John Williams. I was chatting with Allen when Bob shouted urgently for me to follow as he ran to John's van. We picked up two wheels and next stop was the grid, as the riders had been given just a few minutes to change to wets after a sudden downpour. Wedged on a crowded grid, between the best riders in the country, I helped Bob change the wheels on John's RG500, thinking: '*Should I be here?*' I suppose I was already part of the furniture however, '*You know, the bloke with the camera, from the press?*' Indeed, at the end of that meeting, for reasons long forgotten, I had to get home as quickly as possible and got offered a lift from Derek Huxley, who'd already ridden in the 250 event. He was doing development work on the prototype Cotton 250 tandem twin he'd use later that season to beat Mike Hailwood's long-standing lap record taken on the Honda six. I can't remember if he was on the Cotton that day, but I certainly remember the driving. His Transit van had no lights and he was in a hurry to get home before dark. It was white knuckles all the way, from Lincolnshire to Cheshire.

I too seemed to know everyone in the paddock – I suppose this is how it always happens - and by chance, not long after, I was talking to Charlie Williams. I happened to mention that I played squash and, as he expressed an interest in learning, we arranged to play a game. However, Charlie failed to turn up and rang me the next day, full of apologies, *'I crashed my car on the way, can we reschedule the game?'* Needless to say within a couple of games Charlie was a much better player than I'd ever be. That's a racer's fitness and hand/eye coordination for you, though evidently not when behind the wheel. In terms of name dropping I'd also see Bill Smith regularly around the circuits. I'd known him for years, but now as part of the racing fraternity I tried quizzing him on some racing specifics. He'd always avert my enquiries however, starting by saying, *'How are your mum and dad?'* I'd always forget that he went to school with my mum and was a fellow Hoole businessman like dad. He wouldn't let me forget my roots, nor my station, I had to earn my stripes. I suppose I was just Joe Public to someone of his standing, which would have been confirmed if he saw the type of motorcycle I now rode.

I no longer had access to gratis Superbikes and with my DT125 getting somewhat tired I'd already moved it on. I'd been impressed by a little Honda SL125 four-stroke I'd seen being ridden around Llyn Brenig, on Denbigh Moor, so bought a brand new trail version, the TL125. As I'd expected, it was great off-road, but I discovered to my cost that it was a little too focussed; although it had lights it wasn't great on the road. The tiny seat and very low gearing didn't help and it was clear that the bike had really been designed to be ridden standing up. I had a few rides on the local tracks and paths, but as both Steff and Dave's trail riding dropped off around the same time, I lost a lot of enthusiasm and decided to opt for something entirely road biased. An MZ TS250 cropped up, similar to one that I had purchased new some years earlier, so I ran that for a while, until the tell-tale rumbling of main bearings on their way out persuaded me to sell it on. I then bought the Honda CG125 I used to commute to Tom's and it was a bike I had a lot of respect for. However, one day visiting Bob White's, I noticed that he had an old British bike in the corner. My curiosity was aroused and it turned out to be a Triumph twin: a 3TA 350cc. It was complete and in fair condition for its age and such was the value of old British bikes at the time, i.e. next to nothing, that Bob offered me a straight swap for my CG125. He even said that I could take the Triumph straight away, *'We can sort out the paperwork later.'* We've all done it, had an offer we can't turn down dangled in front of us, and I bit. I bought it on an impulse and regretted it almost immediately: it was horrible. For whatever reason, this particular Triumph had a noisy, gutless and vibratory engine that made the CG125 feel sophisticated in comparison. It also didn't handle and had appalling brakes. While I'm sure that with a little time, effort and expertise - none of which I possessed just then - the bike could have been sorted, I needed reliable day-to-day transport. That night I worried what Bob would say if I returned the Triumph and asked for my Honda back? That is if he hadn't sold it already. Next day Bob didn't bat an eye. He probably knew he was pulling a fast one, he was fine. The Honda was soon regularly clocking up thirty-four miles a day again, until I was lured into another deal.

A month after starting at Tom's there was a new arrival in the showroom: Yamaha's new SR500 four-stroke single. In red and black, it looked fantastic but was sadly way beyond my wallet. The Sales Manager thought otherwise however and persuaded me that with a generous trade in on my CG, the monthly payments would be easily affordable, even on my lowly wages. Before I knew it, I had signed on the dotted line and it was only when riding home that anxiety set in, *'What will Steff have to say?'* I needn't have worried. All she was interested in was the key, so she could have a go.

The SR was a lovely bike, with that big-single sound, though not having the long stroke and heavy flywheels of a typical British single, it didn't quite pull from zero revs as I'd hoped. It was still slim, light and fun to ride though, once it was running that is: starting was an issue. From cold it was generally OK. There was a little window in the cam cover and the engine had to be eased over until a mark on the camshaft appeared in this window, indicating that the piston was in the optimum position for starting. A healthy kick would then usually start the bike. When the engine was warm but not fully hot however, starting was a very hit and miss affair. I was left in a sweaty heap by the side of the road on many occasions. Overall though, I enjoyed my time with the Yamaha, especially at the 1978 TT where, being one of the very first to appear on British roads, it always drew a crowd. It was a bit of a novelty and it grew on me. Indeed I would have kept it were it not for Tom advising me to sell it in the Autumn: I was in line for a company bike. The SR500 went to one of Tom's mechanics, but before it did I put together a quick article on the bike as they were still a rarity on the street. I sent it off to the editor of Motorcycle Sport, with some photographs, as while the magazine was considered by some to be stuffy and a bit dated I admired the intelligent writing and the magazine's variety. I'd become a regular reader, so was delighted when my article was published, even if there was no forthcoming fee.

You might already have asked yourself, 'Why didn't he consider pursuing a career in journalism seriously?' As it was true, I had a pretty good CV and, as the response from Motorcycle Sport indicated, someone other than the Cheshire Observer must have thought that I could write. The thing was that although I really enjoyed writing, and still do, I only ever considered it to be a hobby. I also had my suspicions that the money wasn't great, which Motorcycle Sport's lack of payment only confirmed. I probably didn't have the self-confidence to take the leap into full-time journalism at the time either, though I didn't seem to be able to get away from a keyboard.

A while after I had left the Observer, they got in touch with me again, asking if I could do a one off. They had received an invitation to a Honda test day at Donington Park and not wanting to turn them down they wondered if I could fill in. A quick check with Tom got me the appropriate day off and the paper sent me all the details. Basically, Honda was assembling its test fleet for the press to sample and when the paperwork arrived, I discovered that there were actually two tickets, one intended for a photographer. I hadn't thought of that and as I knew that the Observer were unlikely to help out so far from home I asked my instructor friend, Martin Tunnicliffe if he would like to come. He jumped at the chance and the day itself proved well-organised, with a large range of machines available to try on the track.

As I hadn't ridden around Donington Park before, I chose what I thought would be a mild mannered machine to start with and a good benchmark against which to judge my SR500: Honda's FT500 flat-track-styled single. Sure enough, it seemed docile and forgiving, an ideal tool on which to learn the circuit. I tootled around steadily, building my speed up as I went and while the bike was pleasant enough, after the SR500 the geometry seemed more suitable to a trail bike than the out and out roadster the FT500 claimed to be. Like many Japanese singles it seemed to have solved the big problem of the old British thumpers, read vibration, but it had little or no low-down torque. It made the SR500 feel like a real stump-puller in comparison. The FT needed to be revved hard in order to make progress, which begged the question, *'What's the point?'* Was it any different, or could it do anything differently, from one of their existing fours or twins?

In its defence it was targeted at the American market – hence the styling – and it probably wasn't the best bike for the track, which I can't say I really took to either. The first right hander, Redgate, seemed to go on forever, tightening as it went whilst I couldn't seem to find the right line downhill through Craner Curves. What made it worse was the large number of other journalists that were on track at any given time. The fast ones were no trouble. They knew where they were going and seemed to have picked the faster bikes anyway; they cruised past on the right lines and had it all under control. It was the slower riders who were the problem, those *'journalists'* who were probably happier behind a typewriter than a pair of handlebars. Some of these people were *names* from national publications but coming up behind them I'd

The SR500 on the Island. It generated a surprising amount of interest for a single

seen better riding while carrying out novice CBT training. I never knew when they would brake, if they'd brake at all, or where they would position themselves for a corner. I suppose I should have had some sympathy, remembering what I'd been like around Oulton Park on that first Norton Commando test, but these blokes were meant to be professionals, they were getting paid.

I picked out Honda's new CBX550 for my next ride and as Martin took pictures we were approached by a rider in Honda leathers. I recognised him immediately and put two and two together when he put his arm around the shoulder of the unsuspecting Martin and led him off, like a lamb to the slaughter. I only knew what was about to happen as I had seen TT winner Alex George, for it was he, circulating around Donington at high speed *with a pillion passenger*. That was the treat that Martin was about to endure. I say endure as, whilst I was riding the 550, Alex George with Martin gripping him for all that he was worth lapped me *twice* in the space of about six laps. In my defence I was only just getting to grips with the CBX, which was an incredibly small and compact bike compared with the old CB550F it was replacing. The handling was more positive too and the revvy engine really suited the race track. The nature of the engine might have made it a bit frantic on the road, though probably not as frantic as Martin. As I arrived back in the paddock he and Alex pulled in too. They shook hands as Martin leapt off, but by the time I got to him it was clear he was still a gibbering wreck. He was literally shaking from head to foot, as I'm sure I would have been. Martin had little or no idea what had just happened to him and when I explained that he had just had the privilege of riding pillion to a TT winner, what little colour was left rapidly drained from his face.

Memory fails me, but I think I rode only a couple more bikes after the CBX before calling it a day. Some riders' obvious lack of ability scared me: enough was enough. I'm sure that poor old Martin never forgot the day, but oddly it was the opposite for me. There were no bikes which really stood out. The ones I tested were superbly functional, but entirely forgettable, there was nothing which would have tempted me. Had the variety of the last three years simply spoilt me, or had the Japanese simply run out of ideas?

The late spring and early summer of 1978 was a great time for me. I was living and breathing motorcycles all day, every day, and getting paid for it. Under Tom Loughridge's watchful eye I was learning the ins and outs of the trade and trying my best to take it all in. In the workshop I was happy doing basic servicing and the building of new bikes as they were un-crated, as I would have been too slow and ponderous at this stage to have taken on full engine rebuilds. I also think that I was more tolerated than welcomed in the workshop by the mechanics. I'm sure that they saw me as *'Tom's favourite'* and that I was perhaps there to spy on them. Sarcastic comments if they came didn't bother me though, I refused to rise to the bait; the mechanics soon got bored with that game, gave up and got back to their jobs.

In contrast I found working in the stores to be quite easy. There was a Cardex system to show the location and stock levels of all items and I soon got the hang of it. The star of the stores was the storeman, *Brian the Snail*. He was a character from the past really: in his forties, still

Tom at work on the shop lathe. Most dealers wouldn't have had anything like this

living at home with his mum and smoking like a chimney. Brian had slicked back *'rocker-style'* hair from the '50s drape suit era and always wore a collar and tie under his blue Honda storeman's coat, the top pocket of which was always full of pens. Despite appearances, Brian was a fast rider though, eschewing British classics more in line with his image and always liking to have the latest, fastest bikes. In that, he was totally up to date, which was more than could be said for his sales patter. If asked by a customer what was the difference between a cheap polycarbonate crash helmet and a top-of-the-range Bell full-face, for example, he would simply say, *'The price.'* If a customer asked for a specific item such as an NGK B7HS spark plug, or an 8mm bolt, Brian would always ask the unnecessary question, *'What bike's it for?'* usually getting a quizzical look in response. He had many odd ways, including an infuriating habit of randomly over-ordering spares, which could have hilarious consequences. On one of Tom's rare visits to the back of the stores, he re-appeared and asked Brian why he had forty-eight left-hand mirrors for Honda C50s in stock. Brian instantly became flustered and tried to get out of it by saying that he hadn't. So Tom dragged him back to see the evidence with his own eyes, waving a mirror in his face, as Brian became a gibbering, stammering idiot. Tom stormed off in despair, with Brian simply saying, 'Oh dear.' This scenario would be repeated at least once a month, with a variety of different spares, though despite everything, everyone loved Brian. He was a one off though, through expansion, he soon became two.

A young girl called Mandy was taken on to manage clothing sales, while helping Brian in the stores. Mandy may have been short in stature but she was extremely well endowed in other areas. Once a male customer was in front of her, they wouldn't be able to take their eyes off her and, consequently, she could sell them anything. Mandy was well aware of her attributes and used them to her advantage. As word got around about the new girl in the shop, clothing sales went through the roof. Despite the age difference I think that Brian saw Mandy as a substitute for his mum at work. Though he had a lifetime of experience in comparison, he started asking Mandy's advice on everything. As such she would boss him about mercilessly and he was willing putty in her hands. Mind you, she wasn't the only member of the family working there. Mandy's dad, Bill, worked part time as required, building bikes as they were un-crated.

An ex-merchant seaman, he was a huge bear of a man and the salt of the earth. He wasn't necessarily the fastest on the uptake though. If a joke was told he would always laugh later than anyone else as it took a while to register. He wasn't without his faults either. If any defects were found on a newly assembled bike, e.g. indicators wired up incorrectly, or similar, Bill would be sent for. He'd then go through this ritual of closely inspecting some part or other before standing back to convincingly and categorically declare, 'No, it's not one of mine'. The fact that he built ninety percent of all the new bikes never seemed to occur to him. Bill was also paid on a per-bike basis, so he liked to assemble them as quickly as he could. This wasn't fundamentally a problem, though I noticed when Bill had completed a build, he would often go over to the waste bin and there quickly followed a metallic tinkling. One day, simply out of curiosity, I unobtrusively wandered over to the bin and found that it was full of brand new washers. These should have been on the recently assembled bike, so I had a quiet word, *'Tom doesn't need to know if it doesn't happen again.'* It was never a problem after that.

Even more than the workshop I enjoyed working on the sales floor. Selling bikes came naturally and, being obsessed by motorcycles, I had no need to learn the performance figures and specs; I already knew them. My road testing also gave me firsthand knowledge of many of the current models, so I could give advice based on actual experience, not theory. There was only one problem: the Sales Manager obviously didn't like me. He saw me as reasonably intelligent and too friendly with Tom, so considered me to be a threat. I wasn't, I was destined to manage the new branch, I'd soon be out of his hair. None the less he did his best to get the mechanics to side with him against me though ultimately I didn't really care; it was a short-term problem. The Sales Manager was always pleasant to me if Tom was around however, he was sly, so I hoped that Tom was aware of this aspect of his character as he appeared to trust him implicitly otherwise.

I mentioned at the very beginning that when I first visited Tom's workshop I was massively impressed. Only when I began to work in it however did I realise what a fantastic work environment he'd created. The workshop was roomy, clean and bright, featuring high quality ramps and board after board of special tools. The mechanics at the time didn't seem to appreciate it, though compared to the dark, cramped and ill-equipped places where they'd worked before, Tom's was a palace. The over-used cliché, *'You could eat your dinner off the floor'* was almost true, but how did said mechanics show their appreciation for Tom's investment? They moaned, behind Tom's back of course. At great expense, Tom had installed a massive exhaust extraction system. This was made up of a roof-level ducting system with rubber pipes which dropped down by each bike ramp. When a mechanic wanted to run a bike, for example when synchronising carburettors, he was supposed to connect the pipes to the silencers and turn the extractor fans on, so the harmful exhaust fumes would

Exhaust extractors on a Suzuki RE5. A bike I now kick myself for not asking to ride

be safely removed from the building. Of course, this was extra hassle so, if they thought that Tom wasn't around, they wouldn't connect it, though woe betide them if Tom suddenly appeared in the workshop as he would raise the roof.

And he did appear, unannounced, as he was immensely proud of the workshop and would often come in with a potential customer in tow. He thought that seeing the fantastic investment that he had made in order to ensure that their machine was serviced professionally in future would clinch a deal, but very often it didn't; all that most buyers were interested in was the price. Regardless, it was an unwritten rule that whenever Tom arrived with a customer, the workshop should be clean and tidy. He expected the floor to be swept, that all tools should be hung on their correct boards and that there should never be any litter on the floor. Also, even on the hottest of days, he expected mechanics to be wearing their corporate overalls. Tom had high standards and, to be honest, some of the mechanics couldn't see the point. Eventually, those who didn't buy-in to Tom's ethos left and they were probably happier back working in less demanding, back-street garages, even if that seemed a bit short sighted to me. Tom also looked after the professional development of staff, long before this became the norm. At no little cost to himself, he sent us all on manufacturers' training courses though, believe it or not, some even moaned about that. The showroom walls were proudly hung with the certificates gained, although that eventually stopped. Honda poached Tom's star mechanic. They'd seen the quality of his work on one of their service courses and Tom thought that was a little bit off.

Back to the 1978 TT, the build up was frantic, both through assisting Allen and dealing with what was going on in the shop. Steff and I were especially glad that we had arranged our ferry tickets and accommodation in good time however as, when it was announced that Mike Hailwood was to come out of retirement, bookings went through the roof. Everyone of that generation claims to have been on the Island in 1978 and the attendance did have to be seen to be believed. Our early bookings came with another benefit too. Tom and Charlie Williams went over to the Island for practice week so, in theory, I shouldn't have been able to go, or not until the race week proper at least, as someone had to look after the shop. However, as I had booked our sailings well before I'd started work at Tom's, myself, Steff and the SR500 were all travelling the week before as well.

People rail about the problems booking ferry tickets today, but to be honest they haven't got a clue! In those days, you didn't buy a ticket for a particular sailing to the Island, you simply got a ticket for a particular day, turned up and then observed the ridiculous rituals of a monopoly at work. The first was the practice of having, in the laughable interests of 'safety', your petrol drained – i.e. robbed - from your fuel tank in front of your very eyes. God knows how much it was worth and where it went, but I doubt that it was ever declared to the Inland Revenue! In our case, living close to the ferry terminal, we only had a very small amount stolen, before we joined the huge queue of bikes and waited… and waited. Every so often, a ferry would come in and start to load which would result in bikes being frantically fired up to be moved only inches forward. This happened a number of times over the next few hours before, eventually, we were able to board. My main recollection of the crossing was the conversation. Everyone was talking about Mike Hailwood's return, with the consensus being that no one expected him to win; everyone just hoped that he wouldn't get hurt. The swell of goodwill was amazing.

At the quay we disembarked then went through the other ritual, of joining the queue for petrol at Quarter Bridge. Once fuelled, we bypassed the capital entirely, knowing how busy and noisy Douglas can be. Steff and I had booked into a hotel in Port St. Mary in the south of the Island and as it turned out we had chosen well; the Perwick Bay Hotel - sadly long gone - was in a superb location, overlooking the sea. It was the peaceful haven that we had hoped for and we slept like logs before riding into Douglas the following morning to find Allen at the Douglas Bay Hotel.

It seemed it had been an eventful practice week. He and Tony had taken part in the racing at Jurby, an old airfield circuit in the north of the Island, where they had been leading the race on the last lap when the outfit holed a piston. Ever vigilant, Bob White had noticed a puff of smoke from one of the expansion chambers so knew which cylinder was to blame. Once the engine was stripped the fault was traced not to a piston however but to a defective ignition coil, which was replaced in time for TT practice.

During qualification Allen noticed some very strange handling and back at the garage it was discovered that all bar one of the frame tubes to the headstock had snapped! Luckily there was time to find a blacksmith who fabricated a strengthening plate and Ron Williams, from Maxton Engineering, brazed it all in place. The outfit was good to go again and once back Allen and Tony said that they had qualified without too much difficulty. That was an understatement however. Bill Smith popped round shortly after and said that he had been talking to Kenny Williams, the passenger of World Sidecar Champion Rolf Biland. After that last session, Biland had asked Kenny, *'Who was that guy on the black outfit? He shouldn't have been there!'* Apparently, Biland had passed Allen early in the lap, but when he looked behind him at the Ramsey Hairpin, Allen was still there, right behind him,

With good Suzuki connections and an eye for publicity Bob White, Allen's sponsor at the Chester Suzuki Centre, even managed to borrow Barry Sheene's Formula 750 bike

holding station. Allen would have been chuffed just to have been *noticed* by the World Champion, so this was really something. The prospects for the two sidecar races were looking good, but you never count your chickens at the TT. You don't know what might happen and that was certainly the case with the Formula One race, where we positioned ourselves at Governor's Bridge for Mike Hailwood's return. Despite the huge traffic jams through Douglas, we got a good spot by the wall, as although it was one of the slowest points on the circuit, it allowed us to get a great view. You could feel the buzz of anticipation as we waited for the 'Roads Closed' car to pass and the eerie silence that always followed only served to heighten the tension and anticipation. Unless you've experienced it there is nothing quite like that silence before the first bikes come through and when they did Hailwood looked as if he was touring. The news soon came through however that he was in the lead after his fastest-ever lap at 109.87mph. We all watched and listened in on the radio, as Hailwood gradually caught and then passed his arch rival, Phil Read on the road: the cheers went up all around the circuit. Absolutely everyone had their fingers crossed for Mike and when he crossed the line to win on the Sports Motorcycles Ducati there wasn't a dry eye in the crowd; it was as unbelievable a comeback as could have been achieved. Anyone who was privileged to see that race will, I am sure, never forget it, as while it's been talked up ridiculously over the years, it really was an amazing thing to be part of, and as a spectator you really did feel part.

We avoided Mad Sunday, as they were pulling them out of the hedges in those days, many from ridiculously high speeds. The accidents could be catastrophic and so, unfortunately, they proved on Monday too. Pat Hennen crashed out of the Senior, with life-changing injuries, while chasing Tom Herron for the lead. The outcome in the sidecars was even worse. From the commentary, we knew that there had been a major accident on Bray Hill shortly after the start, but it was not until after the race that we heard the tragic news that Mac Hobson and his passenger Kenny Birch had been killed. Their outfit had hit the wall, while, further down the road, Ernst Trachsel had also died when his outfit developed a mechanical fault and crashed in a separate incident. In those days TT races weren't red flagged, so despite the carnage, the race continued and, unaware of the tragedies, Steff and I waited anxiously for Allen and Tony to arrive, strumming our fingers as the minutes on the clock ticked by. We were never to see them, as the news came through on the radio that they had retired at The Highlander.

When we went to see Allen after the race, we thought he'd be devastated, but he was actually quite philosophical. A piston had broken up in the Yamaha engine but the good news was that it could all be rebuilt in time for Wednesday. That's when the second race was, though the weather forecast was far from promising. As a result we decided to head for the relative shelter of Governor's Bridge again, rather than the exposed Mountain section, and we went early as we had a vested interest in the Junior race too. Charlie Williams was riding the Maxton Yamaha that Tom was sponsoring him on, while Tom himself was out on an almost identical machine. Chas Mortimer won however from Charlie Williams, as Mike Hailwood's bike faltered. Tom had a steady ride, finishing thirty-sixth out of sixty-eight starters, which in a strong field was about as good as he could expect.

We then sat for the sidecar race and as expected the rain arrived. A ten minute delay was announced in order to allow crews to change to wet tyres, which I knew would be plenty of time for Allen: he only had one wet wheel. As Allen and Tony were starting at number 74, I knew that we wouldn't hear about them on the radio commentary, but I listened intently anyway, as they would announce any retirements. As the field came through on the first lap, Rolf Steinhausen and Wolfgang Kalauch were looking strong and I thought that if Allen and Tony arrived somewhere amongst the high fifties, they would be progressing really well. The fast guys continued to stream by but then, suddenly, as number 37 fired into The Nook with a wall of spray coming off all three wheels, I did a double take. Right behind him, in his wheel tracks was……number 74! Allen and Tony had passed approximately thirty-five outfits, in one lap, in the pouring rain.

Other fans around us, who understood what Allen's high number indicated, cheered as well as he went through; our hopes of a top ten finish weren't a pipedream. I know it might sound an exaggeration, but my hands were shaking so much in excitement that all of my photographs from the race are blurred. The high start number meant that the radio commentary still didn't mention Allen and Tony during the rest of the race, but I knew from the numbers they were running with each time they came past that they were doing incredibly well. On the final lap, I counted the leading outfits on the road as they passed us at Governor's Bridge and, amazingly, Allen and Tony were eleventh on the road. They had passed sixty-three outfits and as a result, at the end of the race, there was a quite a delay before the results could be announced.

Normally it's known as soon as the first few bikes have crossed the line what the result is, but the timekeepers needed to factor in Allen and Tony's performance. Sure enough, when the results were announced Steele and Barrow were fourth finishers behind Steinhausen/Kalauch, Mick Boddice/Chas Birks and Jock Taylor/Kenny Arthur. The garland-ing ceremony even had to be delayed, as Allen was catching Jock Taylor so quickly on corrected time that he came close to snatching third place off the future World Champion.

To say that we were all happy doesn't scratch the surface. To come from seventy-fourth on the road to eleventh and to finish fourth overall, over just three laps was amazing. To do so in dreadful conditions, against world class opposition, and *at your first attempt*, was simply incredible. Those in the know realised the magnitude of Allen and Tony's achievement. It did their reputation no harm at all, but few knew that Allen's generosity could have cost them a podium place. In the first race Rolf Steinhausen retired with a holed piston. He was also based out of the Douglas Bay hotel and he had been showing the piston around saying, *'Benzine, benzine'* - meaning that he thought it was poor petrol that was the cause of his problem. Allen and Bob saw it, then showed Rolf the piston from their own engine, following the Jurby breakdown. The symptoms looked identical and they convinced the German that an ignition coil was at fault. There were no spare coils to be had, but Allen had one and he gave it to Steinhausen who of course went on to win.

From seventy-fourth on the road to fourth place overall. What an achievement

Chapter 11
Dirty Deals, Death and the Regulars

Back on the mainland the Cheshire County Council Rider Scheme continued to successfully train a significant number of learner riders as, in addition to the scheme that I ran in Chester, there were other centres throughout the county. They were all organised on similar lines and of course, it was all too good to last. It was likely that compulsory training would soon be introduced and there were rumours that training in Cheshire was to be handed over to a national scheme, known as *'Star Rider'*, of which we'd never heard. I tackled Len Williams on this, but he was as angry as me, *'It's all been decided at County level, it's completely out of our hands.'* He added that a meeting was to be arranged where the Chief Road Safety Officer for Cheshire would explain how 1. The new scheme would work and 2. How the existing instructors could get involved. I was wondering what to do about this when I read an article in Motor Cycle News which explained that the same thing was happening all over the country; successful local training schemes were being swallowed up by Star Rider without any discussion, fact-finding or consultation at all.

Like many, the famous stunt rider Dave Taylor was opposed to the take-overs, so I contacted him through MCN and explained who I was, what was happening and about the meeting which was taking place. Dave asked the date and said, *'I'll be up from London, I'll be there.'* I met Dave in advance, with my police friend Bill Ward who was in charge of the Crewe scheme, and it all went extremely well. The instructors were not in the mood to be told what to do and, when Dave Taylor walked in, the assembled dignitaries from the Road Safety Department were clearly caught off guard; they knew who Dave was and were aware of the publicity his attendance would bring. After listening politely to the Star Rider proposals, Dave Taylor took the floor and spoke very eloquently about the national situation and the stupidity of replacing successful, volunteer-run, organisations with a theoretical, commercial one. The next blow came from Bill Ward and myself. We explained that we were prepared to set up a rival, independent voluntary scheme, to run throughout Cheshire that would be less costly to the Road Safety Department. The instructors present unanimously supported the idea and we dropped in that the Cheshire Police would help with instructor training; Bill Ward had already checked on this. The opposition crumbled. We were basically offering the Road Safety Department an oven-ready, police-endorsed scheme, while removing any administrative burden. What could they say but, 'Yes'? That night, Cheshire Motorcycle Training was born, a scheme which would run successfully for many years and for which we owed Dave Taylor a big thanks. He was a warm-hearted man whose publicity stunts were just that; stunts to bring attention to his one goal, improving motorcycle safety.

The attempted Star Rider coup was perhaps indicative of the times, as the motorcycle trade in general had become extremely cut throat by the end of the 1970s. It was a national phenomenon, but in the Wirral and Chester area in particular there were a lot of dealers and they were all trying to sell essentially the same thing. Tom hoped to persuade customers to buy from us, through the quality of our workshops and our professional approach to after-sales service. It worked for some, but most were only interested in one thing, the price, and that often worked against us. As a matter of principle, we always sold bikes at the official retail price, perhaps throwing in a helmet or rear carrier on a cash deal as a sweetener. Unfortunately for us, many dealers would offer huge discounts; so big that there was scarcely a profit margin at all. How on earth could we compete with that? Well, Tom had an idea.

Most buyers tended to use the dealer's own hire purchase facilities in order to fund their new bikes. In those days, interest rates were high, in the order of fourteen or fifteen percent, but the dealers received a good commission rate from the financiers, so it was in their interest to push the product. Tom worked out that if we kept our interest rates really low, by taking little or no commission, people who bought from us at full retail price would actually pay *less* per month than those who got a discount, as these discounting dealers charged the highest interest. It was a sound plan, but there was one fatal flaw; people couldn't get their heads round the idea. How could a bike from us

Dave Taylor doing what he was best known for, here riding around the TT circuit

costing (say) £200 *more* than from another dealer cost them £10 per month *less*? Don't get me wrong, we did OK from this scheme but we lost a good number of customers as they simply couldn't get their heads around the basic concept of interest! That level of financial naivety was not uncommon, so they'd never have understood what Tom tried next.

An extra complication when trying to sell bikes were the antics of one particular dealer. Even when certain models were in short supply, he seemed to have unlimited access. He obviously didn't enjoy seeing us making a living out of selling motorcycles however as he had a cunning plan to severely curtail our supply. It worked like this: this dealer wouldn't sell to us, instead supplying any number of smaller, un-franchised outfits, usually bicycle shops, on a sale or return basis. As these shops had low overheads and didn't have to pay for bikes until they'd been sold, they could sell at unbelievable discounts. Any profit was a good profit for them: it might be a fiver. This practice dented our new bike sales, as it did the sales of other dealers. However, Tom had a plan to get our own back, even if only on a minor scale. It's complicated, but I'll try to explain how, by giving you an actual example. One day, a potential customer arrived in our showroom. He wanted to purchase a certain new bike, but it wasn't a model that we had in stock and was at the time very hard to get hold of through the official importer. An additional problem was that the customer wanted to part-exchange his tatty old 125. Tom had a look at the bike and soon realised that it was in a poor state of repair and virtually worthless. Standing alongside Tom, I knew that we couldn't do a deal, so you can imagine my surprise when Tom asked, *'How much can you afford to pay?'* The buyer replied with an amount indicating that he expected about £200 for his wreck, if he paid us full retail price on the new machine. *'That's it then'* I thought. But no, Tom continued, *'We might be able to do something, but I can't promise. Can you leave the bike with us for a day or two and can you bring the log book in?'* The buyer replied that he could and I was even more puzzled when Tom asked, *'Would you mind if your new bike had about ten miles on it?'* Again, the buyer said there was no problem, and left.

Rather than explain everything twice, Tom asked me to wait a minute as he shouted for one of the mechanics to come up from the workshop. Tom then asked him, *'Does anyone at *** cycle shop know you?'* The answer came back in the negative, so Tom explained that he wanted the mechanic to ride the 125 wreck down to the cycle shop and try to do a deal with it against the new bike, which Tom just happened to know they had in stock. It worked like a dream. To get the sale the other dealer offered far too much on the 125 and as a result we actually made a good profit. We got rid of a real wreck of a swapper and ended up with a happy customer who was none the wiser. Two days later, after we had checked the bike over and swapped the other dealer's number plate for one of ours, the buyer collected his new machine from us. I can't remember how we squared the paperwork for the new registration document, but it must have panned out OK as we managed to pull this stunt off a few more times until we ran out of un-franchised cycle shops selling bikes in our area. I don't *think* that what we did was illegal, and it wasn't our fault that the cycle shops couldn't recognise a wreck when they saw one. After all, we were only trying to make a living, and there's a golden rule in business: never get involved in something you don't understand.

By now motorcycle training was one thing I *did* understand. The new Cheshire Motorcycle Training set-up was established and Dennis Carter-Wardell – he of the Silk test - became my right hand man. His handlebar moustache and clipped turn of phrase gave Dennis away as an ex-RAF Aircraftsman and he would regularly regale us with tales of working on Spitfires on the allies' advance through Italy. As a dyed-in-the-wool sidecar man, his outfit was also very useful as it became a very effective shield from other traffic when he followed a group of first-timers. Visits to Dennis's house were also hugely popular among the unattached, as he had two beautiful but not worldly wise daughters; Dennis did a good job of protecting their virtue.

We had an established roster of instructors but new ones would come on board periodically through a variety of means. On one occasion, a mature Scottish lady called Ann enrolled on the course and every week she was accompanied by a man on a TriBSA: a Triumph engine in a BSA frame. He would disappear during the lesson and return at the end, to escort Ann home. He looked the type, so I asked Ann if her husband would be interested in becoming an instructor. *'Eee luv, he's not me 'usband, he's just the bloke I live with!'* He was soon one of the most conscientious and reliable instructors. Another time a cheerful chap turned up on an ex-police BMW and offered his services. His name was Jim Shawcross, and he proved invaluable, as he worked as a mechanic for the police in Chester, servicing their patrol vehicles. He never seemed to take anything too seriously but always did a good job and was a useful man to have around when it came to checking the roadworthiness of the trainees' bikes. Jim's activities were heavily regulated by his wife however, who he jokingly called the FPO - Fun Prevention Officer – though looking back I perhaps didn't appreciate the efforts people made, nor the quality of the instructors we were able to attract, all of whom still had to go through training themselves. We organised this via Bill Ward and the Cheshire Police. All instructors, no matter how long they had worked for the scheme, had to undergo training, which consisted of being followed by a police motorcyclist who would then give a formal assessment of the ride. You received a certificate and printed hi-viz CMT Instructor vest, which we all wore with pride. There were even occasional perks.

One of these occurred through Bill Smith. He was organising a Honda Test Day where, on the production of a full motorcycle licence, anyone could have a go on any machine from the current Honda range. As the 1970s moved on the market became more and more competitive so, while test rides had been a no-no previously, the Japanese now started actively encouraging road shows of this type. Bill had organised a test route of about ten miles and he wondered if I could provide a team of travelling marshals from the ranks of my instructors. Bill gave us a briefing on what was expected. Riders would be told that they were not allowed to pass us leaders, but when I asked Bill about speed limits he just looked at me and smiled, *'Once out of town, there won't be any police on the route.'* I wondered how he knew, but Bill Smith knew everyone. We had a fun, trouble-free day, riding someone else's bikes as fast as we - and the police - liked.

Unfortunately as 1978 ran into 1979 everything wasn't quite as positive as the rider training. Allen successfully defended his Southern 100 title, with lap and race records and after his great result at the TT he was offered start money to ride in the Ulster Grand Prix. Due to work I couldn't be there, but as it turned out I was glad I wasn't. Expectations were raised when Allen and Tony matched Jock Taylor's lap record from the previous year in practice and Allen was in second place, behind Jock on the final lap of the race. Unfortunately he had to take to the grass to pass a backmarker and, in doing so, a petrol pipe was ripped off the underside of the outfit. Allen was forced to limp to the finish with a spluttering engine and was passed by three outfits in the process, to finish fifth. It was a memorable performance, for all the wrong reasons, but worse was to come. Tom was also racing and he 'phoned me at the shop, to tell me how he had got on. He added that local rider John Williams had taken a minor spill, so he was off to see him in hospital. The next morning I got a tearful phone call from Tom's wife, Ann, to tell me that John had died. Eventually, it transpired that he had a rare undiagnosed underlying condition which led to complications and ultimately caused his death. Needless to say, the racing community in the North West was devastated. John was a regular visitor to the shop and I had got to know him well. Like many very talented people, he played down his achievements and appeared

Stan Woods taking possession of a TZ750. Equally interesting however was Alan Dugdale (left) as Alan had quite a back story himself. Having been invalided out of racing in 1965 he came back to win the Senior Classic Manx Grand Prix in 1986

to be just a likeable, ordinary bloke. It was a subdued racing season after that, though it didn't affect Allen's results. At an autumn meeting at Oulton Park, Allen and Tony had a flying start and led for three laps before being overtaken by Roy Hanks and Dave Wells. Second place was a great result, there was no disgrace in being beaten by Roy Hanks, but it was made even better by the fact that the third place outfit was that of World Champion, George O'Dell. Allen also won the Aintree Championship and finished in the top ten in the British Sidecar Championship, a result that meant he qualified for the following year's World Championships. There wasn't the money to make that happen, but it was still some achievement. The icing on the cake was being mentioned in the prestigious annual Motocourse book, for his efforts at the TT.

As winter approached, Tom discouraged me from riding to and from work and I reluctantly gave in, using the firm's Honda Civic for my commute in the worst of the weather. I'd sold the Yamaha SR500 to one of the mechanics, Dave, and took a bike in part exchange: an old Honda CB125. It was very tatty, but looks could be deceptive; it had a big bore kit, raising capacity to about 160cc and - would you believe - a Yoshimura camshaft. The bike would rev and rev and was far quicker than any 125 Honda should ever have been. The price to pay was vibration and excessive oil consumption but even so, it was a fun little bike when I wasn't in the Civic, and it humbled a few much bigger machines.

The Honda was just a stop-gap, though I honestly hadn't given much thought to my next bike. Brian the storeman, mechanic Jack and bike-builder Bill all had Suzuki GS750s and reckoned that they were the bike to have. At the time they probably were, so I followed suit and a red GS750 was prepared. However, it sat in the showroom for some time as I waited for the weather to improve. I still had my little Honda, to ride in the slush, sleet and snow and to be honest that winter was to prove no place to be on two wheels. It was awful, particularly as one Thursday late in December, I arrived back to find that Steff wasn't home.

She'd told me that she would be visiting her mother on the way back, but hours later, when she still hadn't arrived on her CG125 I started to get concerned. We didn't yet have a telephone, so Steff couldn't contact me, but when there was a knock on the door I simply thought that she must have forgotten her keys. When I opened it, it wasn't her, but my brother Dave, *'Steff's had an accident, she's in Chester Royal Infirmary'*. I found her sitting up in bed, chatting to the ward sister. A mixture of shock and relief welled up inside me so I immediately had to go outside for a breath of fresh air, as I heard cries of, *'typical man'* from all the nurses. A Ford Capri had pulled out in front of her and the tibia and fibula in her right leg were broken. She would be having an operation that evening to re-align the bones and as she knew the staff well - she worked at the hospital – she was able to get herself allocated to Mr. John Walkden. She considered him the best orthopaedic surgeon around, an opinion that was shared by Charlie Williams, Stan Woods and all the other local racers; they all had their injuries looked after by him. Steff took this all in her stride, along with the long period of immobility, but unfortunately 1979 didn't start any better.

One evening, after work, we all set off for home, Mandy on her Honda 400/4 and her dad, Bill, on his Suzuki GS750. Once we were out of the 30mph limit it was no surprise that Mandy and Bill steadily pulled away, even if I was on my 125cc *Yoshimura*. They were soon out of sight. A couple of miles down the dual carriageway however, I came across a terrible scene. Mandy's bike was lying across the road in front of me and behind the bike was a car, straddling the road. I quickly stopped, parked my bike and ran forward, expecting to find Mandy underneath the car that had obviously pulled out on her. Thankfully, I heard screaming from the other side, as having been thrown over the top of the car by the force of the impact, Mandy was lying in the road. The noise was horrible, but it told me that she was alive and conscious. My Boys' Brigade First Aid training kicked in and luckily it seemed Mandy had no more than a badly broken wrist. Her main concern was that she had chipped a tooth and that this would affect her looks. The main concern of the onlookers was that her dad was going to pull the driver out and kill him! The culprit wisely stayed put in his car, with the door closed and the window up, until the police arrived. Mandy was eventually taken to hospital and thankfully had no other injuries. Even so, her wrist took some time to heal.

That had been quite a succession of events, but just when I was thinking that things couldn't get any worse, it began to snow and snow and snow. Anyone who experienced the winter of 1978/9 will remember that the snow was around for weeks. Where we lived in North Wales was quite high up, so we suffered more than most. Several feet of snow lay for weeks and it was constant sub-zero temperatures. Despite having use of the car, for over a week it was actually impossible to move on our estate on four wheels. Despite the Arctic conditions, I still got to work on my little Honda every single day and I actually quite enjoyed those rides. The roads were deserted and it gave me a chance to practise my green lane riding skills. Of course, the journey to work took twice as long as usual, but at least I got there, where I had to look at my brand new Suzuki GS750 sitting in the showroom waiting for better weather to arrive. It was a grim old period but one bright point was a fundraising night organised by the TT Supporters Club. Plenty of local racers attended the film show and

I remember as we walked in Irishman Tommy Robb, the ex-works Honda Grand Prix rider, rushed to get Steff - still on crutches - a chair and put her in pride of place. It made Tommy a friend for life.

As a result of John Williams' death, Steff and Mandy's accidents and of course the weather, we were all feeling quite low at Tom's in early 1979. Things were soon to brighten up though, with the arrival of Colin Atkinson. Anticipating a busy spring, Tom felt that we could do with an extra pair of hands in the workshop. He knew that Colin was a useful lad who could turn his hand to anything so convinced him to join, though for a limited period only. Colin had other plans, such as working in the shipyards of Hamburg and crossing the Sahara Desert in his Land Rover. He was that type of man, a free spirit. His arrival lifted everyone's mood. He was, and still is, a real character with a quick wit and intelligence to match. With a wild mop of curly black hair, a black beard and mad, staring eyes, Colin wasn't someone who you could easily forget. The fact that he was a real grafter and a great problem-solver, who could communicate well with everyone from an experienced motorcyclist to an old lady with a problem on her moped, made him a great asset. Colin's presence galvanised the workshop, which was important. There had been numerous changes of staff since my arrival and although he wasn't technically in charge, Colin could organise and make things happen.

We had two new mechanics, both called John. The eldest and most experienced was John Banks, known to all as 'Banksy'. He was a good mechanic and skilled engine builder who was quite malleable if you approached him right. Banksy could let customers rub him up the wrong way though, so we tried to keep them away. The other John was known universally as 'The Mumbler' as more often than not it was impossible to understand what he was actually saying. Banksy took this young lad, who was learning his trade, under his wing and they worked well together. Although the Sales Manager hid his feelings, I could tell that he was not happy. The original mechanics who had now left had been allies of his, but the new staff had no such allegiance. He felt that he was losing control of things and the fact was that I didn't trust him. I looked forward to the opening of our new branch, which would inevitably split us up. I had what it took to manage the shop, not least due to the *'customer relations'* skills I'd developed through the many interesting characters that we met.

One regular visitor to our shop was a huge bear of a man who, as a coalman, was invariably filthy and would leave a trail of coal dust behind him as he crossed the showroom floor. He was the bane of Brian the storeman's life, as Brian was terrified of him. The coalman's technique was always the same. He would bark out his spares order and Brian would dutifully go into the stores, fetch the items, put them on the counter and announce the price i.e. £12.50 or whatever. The coalman would then grab the parts, disdainfully throw a ten pound note or similar on the counter and say, *'That's all they're worth!'* before turning around and marching out of the shop. Eventually, Brian was banned from serving the coalman. He refused to confront him and we

The local trade was full of characters. TT racers Eddie Roberts, Bill Smith and Steve Murray around a racer of unknown provenance, decked-out in classic, period, *Honda-Style* colours

couldn't afford for the shop to be seen as an easy touch. From then on he'd nervously shout for Mandy in the clothing department, or for me, as we were made of sterner stuff; we'd keep hold of the spares until we had our hands firmly on the correct cash.

Two of my favourite customers were Alfred and Cyril. They were a pair of quiet, unassuming gents in their sixties. Alfred owned a large department store in Liverpool and was reputed to be a peer of the realm, whilst Cyril was a High Court judge. They were pillars of the establishment, but also avid motorcyclists. On their days off they used to potter around the lanes, and go on longer tours, stopping for refreshments at roadside bars and restaurants that they passed. On one such trip the pair were riding in the Lake District and they stopped at an upmarket pub to order lunch and drinks. When they entered the bar, the landlord took one look at them in their helmets and wax cottons, and announced, *'We don't serve motorcyclists here.'* Alfred and Cyril were outraged, but were far too civilised and genteel to make a fuss. They promptly left, without a word, but over the next couple of weeks they told me that they hatched a plan. They returned to the pub, this time travelling in *'civvies'*, by Bentley, along with a number of their well-heeled friends in cars of a similar ilk. On arrival, they were cordially greeted by the landlord and they proceeded to order a huge round of very expensive drinks. Once the impressive array was on the bar and the cost was announced by the smilingly expectant landlord, Alfred said, in a loud, cultured and perfectly clipped, calm voice, *'Oh, I'm sorry, I forgot, you don't serve motor-cyclists, do you?'* On cue, the entire party turned and left, leaving a speechless landlord staring at the drinks, untouched on the bar. It was a moral victory, beautifully orchestrated, which demonstrated how to go about things in a polite and civilised way.

Alfred was obviously good at this, as when Steff and I were at the TT in 1980, we were riding up from Port St. Mary to Douglas, when we spotted him sitting on his bike at the side of the road, obviously enjoying the view. We turned around and rode back to him as I was surprised to see him on his bike; I thought that he had said that he had bought a day ticket. He had, but he turned up for the ferry on his bike anyway, paid for it, and as there was nothing in the rules that specifically said that bikes couldn't be taken on day trips, he was allowed to sail. I'm sure that the loophole was soon closed, though Alfred could still probably have talked his way through. He had the skills of soft persuasion, but he wasn't the only customer who seemed to get away with things.

Another was a chap who came into the shop and announced that he would like to buy a sidecar outfit. His name was Bowie, so of course, we instantly christened him 'David'. Mr. Bowie was a short, stocky man who had the thickest lenses in his glasses that I had ever seen. I hoped that he could see well enough to actually ride a bike and when he asked if we could supply a sidecar outfit I tried not to display my horror, 'That would be no problem.' We duly ordered a Squire sidecar with fittings for a new Honda CB550 that he'd requested. Banksy had experience of sidecar fitting, so he set it up, toe-in, angle of dangle and all that, but it was only then that we found out that Mr. Bowie had never driven an outfit before; he didn't even know the theory. So guess who got the teacher's job? From my extensive knowledge - a week on the Dugdale's demonstrator XS650 combo - I painstakingly explained the cornering techniques, 'Your right hand is your best friend' and all the rest of it, while demonstrating them with Mr. Bowie sitting firmly in the chair. His own first attempts at driving were frightening, for the passenger at least, as that was me. Let's just say that he didn't come across as a natural and I fully expected to get a call later in the day, to pick up a mangled outfit; it never happened. Mr. Bowie returned at regular intervals to have the outfit serviced or to pick up the odd spare part and he always seemed very happy with his purchase. The adage, 'You shouldn't judge a book by its cover' rang in my ears, though in some cases the cover was a bit of a clue.

A regular visitor was our next door neighbour, antiques dealer Mr. Hyde. He must have been well into his seventies and his dishevelled appearance showed that sartorial elegance wasn't a priority. He always wore the same old suit, usually with his pyjamas on underneath and he had tobacco stains and fag ash in his unkempt beard; you get the picture. Mr. Hyde would often come in but it was never anything to do with motorcycles. He would ask for help in lifting furniture into the back of his battered Volkswagen Variant and frequently his visits were simply to ask what time, or even what day, it was; the profits of the antique trade clearly didn't extend to the cost of a watch. One visit and question was more memorable than most though. I heard an almighty screech of tyres outside, but thankfully no sound of a collision. Minutes later, a visibly shaken Mr. Hyde appeared and, in all seriousness, he asked me, *'What side of the road do we drive on in this country son?'* Before departing the same way he'd come in. It was a wonder how he survived, both on the road and in business, but somehow he always did.

At the other end of the economic spectrum a man who was obviously worth a bob or two arrived in the showroom one day. Although he lived locally, we couldn't recount ever seeing him before, and he came in solely to announce that while he was due to go to the TT the next day, he had a bit of a problem, *'Would you be able to look at it?'* An hour later, there was a very distinctive howl as he arrived outside, and on what a bike. It was an MV 750 four that had been converted to chain drive and also breathed on by MV Agusta tuning legend, Arturo Magni. Even though it was misfiring, the MV still sounded beautiful and the problem turned out to be minor: a couple of blocked carburettor jets, which were soon fixed. Then, the sound was truly magnificent and we all stood listening to it as the delighted customer rode it away.

We didn't usually see bikes like that round here, but obviously the run in to the TT was always a busy time. We weren't far from the ferry and invariably, just before race week, a dapper, elderly gentleman, with a suit and tie under his riding gear would appear at the counter, to see Tom. He was Albert Moule, the distinguished Manx Grand Prix and TT racer, with leader board finishes in both events - a bit of research revealed he had a best of second in the 1947 Junior Manx and eighth in the 1951 Senior TT. After a cup of tea and an hour's chat with Tom, Albert would head for the ferry, cross to the Island and take up his duties, which were now as a Travelling Marshal. I looked out for Albert's distinctive hooped helmet design around the circuit whenever I was there, and I was always amazed at his speed: he'd certainly not lost any of his skills to age. We'd get a lot of old racers in actually. Renowned tuner and racer Terry Shepherd was an occasional visitor. He'd been a regular competitor in the Continental Circus and I really enjoyed listening to his tales of a truly fascinating period; a time when ordinary blokes could go out and do extraordinary things. Another good talker was the Michelin Tyres representative, who used to visit us regularly and had the rare distinction of arriving on his own BMW; most reps by the late 1970s were in a car or van. He was Vernon Edwards, a good friend of Tom's, and he would regale us with stories of his love of motorbikes, which was obviously in his genes. Vernon's son, Mike *'Spike'* Edwards became a very talented racer, and of course many of the current racers would drop in too. I've mentioned people like Bill Smith, as well as John and Charlie Williams, but the great Irish rider Tom Herron would be a regular as well. He'd often spend time on the Wirral, as one of his sponsors lived locally, so in 1978 in particular

In the 1975 Senior TT Tom Herron came twenty-first. He was third four-stroke home on the Arter Matchless however, and only just behind Barry Ditchburn's works Kawasaki at the line. I'm glad I caught this photo, it's one of Tom's rides which is often forgotten

he would be in and out of the shop. I remember I asked him what it was like racing against Mike Hailwood at the TT that year and he told me that he had found himself behind Hailwood at Quarter Bridge in practice and decided to follow his lines for a while. As they were so strange, Tom said that he nearly abandoned the idea, but he stuck with it and at the end of the session, he found that the lap where he'd followed Mike had been his fastest. He was a lovely, typical, Irish lad, taken from us far too soon.

The winter before, 1978 into 1979, seemed to drag on forever, every day seemed the same. Due to the weather, things at work were very quiet and the days were long and boring. I would sit on my new Suzuki in the showroom, looking out at the snow piled up on the pavements and wondered if I would ever get my new bike home. The weather was still lousy, but I made the decision to tax the Suzuki from April 1st and I'm glad to say, after waiting so long, that the ride home wasn't an anti-climax. Suzuki had done their sums well and had produced a nicely-balanced motorbike, which carried its 492lb weight extraordinarily well. 63bhp would still be healthy today and the GS750 was more sure-footed than the big Japanese bikes that I had tested for the Observer. Japanese bikes were still improving, year on year, and the Suzuki soon fitted me like a second skin. It made short work of the commute to work and was comfortable and effortless to ride. Perhaps it was a little too civilised though, as before long I fitted a Yoshimura 4-into-1 exhaust system that probably did nothing for performance but, oh, did it make a glorious noise.

At home, Steff was straining at the bit to get back on a bike and when her long leg plaster was replaced by a less restrictive one, she decided that she would be able to manage my Honda 125. The beaming smile on her face after a brief ride round the block told its own story and following some rides on the back of the big Suzuki she was sure she'd be OK to go to the TT. Plans were made and as the weather gradually improved, Steff and I had more outings on the GS, often in the company of my cousin Nettie and her husband Graham on his Kawasaki Z1000. Although Steff would have much preferred riding her own bike to riding pillion, it made sense and we rode like this to the first couple of meetings of the season to watch Allen and Tony race. After the successes of 1978, Allen wanted to be even more competitive in 1979, so another outfit was called for. The previous season the top runners had started to use monocoque Windle outfits so Allen bought Bill Hodgkins', though personally I was sad to see the tubular Windle chassis go. It could have still been competitive and this type of outfit was more suited to the road circuits. That's hindsight talking however and there were changes on the engine front too. As a result of Allen and Tony's TT and Southern 100 performances, North Wales Suzuki spares distributor, Bran Bardsley, stepped-in, providing sponsorship in the form a new TZ750 motor. The outfit was painted in the same fantastic black, red and white pattern as 1978 however, though teething troubles meant that the start of the season wasn't the success that we all hoped for. The outfit wouldn't steer properly under braking and was far from competitive. Additionally, the engine had overheating problems, which weren't solved until fitting a completely different radiator.

The Spring was a busy time for everyone and as a result one part of my life sadly ended. You might have thought than when I left the Observer, to work for Tom, that my writing stopped, but oddly it had continued, bar the road tests. The powers that be asked me to keep it going so, for a time, I'd been taking a weekly ride to Chester in order to deliver my ramblings for that week's edition. The problems were two-fold however. Firstly I no longer had the time, while secondly I was now working for one specific dealer, a rival, meaning that other shops - i.e. *advertisers* – would no longer see my writing as objective. They were probably right too, so a few months later the last edition of Motorcycle Scene was published. I'd had a fantastic run with the column, but the time was right to wind it up: I had no regrets. My focus was now one hundred percent on the trade which of course received a huge boost in 1979: Mike Hailwood was riding at the TT again.

Chapter 12
They Think it's all Over.........

TT bookings for 1979 were incredibly high again, but we persuaded Nettie and Graham to come too and were able to get lodgings where we had stayed before. I listened into what was going on during practice week, as Tom and others from the shop had already departed. On the Thursday, just as we were preparing to leave, I tuned into Manx Radio again which was a feat in itself, as reception was very poor from that distance. However as I held the radio to my ear I just about caught the news we all dreaded, '*Allen Steele and Tony Barrow have crashed at Ballaugh Bridge and have been taken to Nobles Hospital.*' There was no easy way of finding out how they were, but Tom rang through to the shop the next day, to say that while Allen and Tony were both battered and bruised, they had largely emerged unscathed. The outfit on the other-hand was a mess, though amazingly they still hoped to race.

Saturday was our busiest day in the shop. I would have to work, so on the Friday Steff got the train to Liverpool and met Nettie and Graham at the quayside. Once in Douglas, Graham ferried Steff, who knew the way to the hotel, and then went back for Nettie. I missed the Saturday Formula One race, where Hailwood could only manage fifth on an ailing machine. I was preoccupied with packing, as on Sunday I rode to Brian the Snail's house as we planned to ride to the ferry together. I was amused to see Brian's mum put his scarf on for him and then give him his packed lunch for the journey. As we left, she gave us a cheery wave and I'm sure that she had a tear in her eye. It was like his first school trip all over again.

On the Monday, we'd decided to watch the first Sidecar race and the Senior from the churchyard at Braddan Bridge. Parking spaces were at a premium, but we managed to squeeze the Suzuki and Graham's Kawasaki down a side road. The 'S' bends at Braddan provided a fantastic viewing point, even if Allen and Tony weren't overly optimistic about their chances; the outfit had been patched together, the handling problems still persisted from the start of the season, and they were both battered and bruised. The beautifully painted fairing now looked a mess as it was covered in filler, prompting Motor Cycle Weekly to caption their photo in the race report, *'Allen Steele and Tony Barrow on their well-worn Yamaha'*. Considering the state of both outfit and crew, a tenth place finish, at a race average of over 95mph wasn't shabby, especially as they finished on the tail of Rolf Biland and Kurt Waltisberg. The race was won at over 102mph by Trevor Ireson and Clive Pollington, just ahead of Dick Greasley and John Parkins. Mick Boddice and Chas Birks were third, but then they always seemed to get on the podium. Nine out of the top ten finishers were on Yamahas, as it was pretty much pointless having anything else by then.

In the Senior race, Mike Hailwood was riding a Suzuki RG500 and, while Mick Grant took an early lead, the pain from a previous North West 200 accident became too much as Hailwood went on to record his fourteenth and final TT win. He set lap and race records in the process, finishing a colossal two minutes ahead of Tony Rutter. It was a great day's racing but as we walked back to the bikes there was an obvious problem: Graham's Kawasaki wasn't there. It took a minute or so for us to register the fact, but it had clearly been stolen. I took Graham to Police Headquarters to report the theft and we then spent ages riding round looking for the bike. Trying to find a fairly common model on the Isle of Man during TT week was, of course, pointless so there we were, just a couple of days into the week with Nettie and Graham with no transport. I ferried everyone back to the hotel and the good news was that once word got around, drinks kept arriving at our table. Tom Loughridge had brought a Honda CB100 in his van as a runabout, so the next morning I rode to his digs with Graham on the pillion and the Honda was duly handed-over. The situation was far from ideal, but at least Nettie and Graham had transport. We watched Wednesday's racing from Signpost, in glorious sunshine, where the Junior race was dominated by Charlie Williams. He smashed the eleven year old lap record, with a lap at 106.83mph and there were a gaggle of 250s behind him that seemed to be nose-to-tail throughout the race. This group consisted of Graeme McGregor, Ian Richards and Chas Mortimer and despite swapping places every lap they finished in that order. It provided a fabulous spectacle, but we were to be disappointed in the second Sidecar race. Allen and Tony failed to finish in a race won by Trevor Ireson and Clive Pollington again. They were followed home by the British Barton Phoenix of Nigel Rollason and Dave Homer, which at least resulted in a bit of flag waving.

We had to return home on the Friday, as I had to be in work on Saturday morning. As such we watched the start of the Classic race from Quarter Bridge and followed that over the radio on the ferry. It was a shame we missed it as it was a classic in every sense of the word. Alex George on the big Honda led for four laps, but Mike Hailwood on his RG500 Suzuki was closing all the time. Hailwood took the lead on the penultimate lap and was 0.8 seconds ahead at the start of the last lap. Alex dug deep though and ultimately won by 3.4 seconds, after Hailwood slowed for a backmarker, George Fogarty - Carl's dad – over the Mountain. At an average speed of 113.08mph, it was the fastest TT race in history, but what people often overlook is the performance of Charlie Williams. He had a fantastic ride into third on his 350cc Maxton Yamaha. We weren't actually there of course, but we were in spirit, listening in to the crackly Manx Radio commentary on the boat as the sound grew gradually fainter.

I didn't manage to get to the Southern 100 races in 1979, where Allen and Tony had to settle for an unsatisfactory third place. After all the handling problems, Allen took the chassis back to Terry Windle to seek his opinion and was surprised when Terry said, *'Ah, it hasn't been right since Bill Hodgkins crashed it',* a crash that Allen knew nothing about! Terry cut the chassis in half and welded in a new main section, after which the outfit steered beautifully. It would have been good to have known the accident story from the start however, as after the repairs the rest of the season featured leader board finishes in a number of races. Overall however the year was something of an anti-climax following the whirlwind of 1978.

During the winter of 1979-80, Tom Loughridge found premises for the much-anticipated second branch in Wallasey, on the north east side of the Wirral. Although quite a small building, it was in a good

Allen and Tony on the 1979 Bran Bardsley sponsored machine. We didn't know that this was to be the last year of the pairing

location and as soon as a lease was agreed Tom started preparing it for a spring opening. The plan at this stage was still for me to go over to manage it, with one of the mechanics coming along to undertake servicing and repairs. As Tom was working on the fixtures and fittings, he put a couple of bikes in the window, just to make it clear what the shop would be selling. We had so many people knocking on the glass to enquire about the bikes that things were looking promising.

As we'd soon be opening and as Tom didn't like to keep company bikes on the books for more than a year, he told me to put my GS750 up for sale and asked me to think about what bike I wanted next. I had a good look around and I took a shine to the beautiful little Laverda Alpino 500 twin. The bike was small and light and, as an Italian, was expected to have great handling. Laverdas won their class in the famous Barcelona 24hr race two years running, and the racer-ised version, the Montjuic, would soon be the thing to have in British Production and Formula II racing. Tom was happy with my choice. An order was put in to Slater Brothers, the Laverda importer, so all I had to do was to wait and to hope that the winter wouldn't be as long as the last one. Steff was now fit enough to ride a bike again and understandably she wanted to move on from her crash damaged CG125 so I decided to surprise her. I bought a brand new Suzuki GSX250 on HP, took the bike home in the van one night and said, '*Steff, can you help me to deliver a bike?*' When she came outside, I opened the back of the van and said, '*Oh look, it's already arrived.*' She was delighted.

As the Laverda's arrival got closer, I became a bit anxious. I had heard that some of the eight-valve twins were having valve and cylinder-head problems and that these weren't isolated cases. I needed a reliable bike above all else, so I talked it over with my boss, '*Tom, I might have a bit of a predicament.*' He understood totally, asked what I'd choose instead and given the much higher mileages I'd now be doing, I plumped for a Suzuki GS1000 instead. What a mistake! I seemed to have forgotten how much bigger the GS1000 was in comparison to the 750 that I had used the year before. It might have had 90bhp on tap, but at 507lbs wet it was heavy, something I'd not noticed riding one lap around Oulton Park to deliver one to Barry Sheene.

I persevered with it for a month or two, but I didn't enjoy it; not least as there was a time lag in the wet, between pulling the lever and when the brakes actually started to work. I was scared of the beast, bit the bullet and told Tom. I needn't have worried. He was quite happy for me to sell it on, there was no shortage of buyers and, in the meantime, I had the use of a second-hand Suzuki GS450 twin. Weighing less than 400lbs the bike was much more to my liking; it had plenty of power and was way more manageable for real world riding. Needless to say when the GS1000 was sold, I plumped for the GS450's replacement, the new four-valve, GSX400 twin. This was a very similar bike, but having four valves per cylinder, it just revved more. I actually preferred the 450, the engine felt more relaxed, but there wasn't really much in it and the 450 wasn't available new anymore. As an aside, on transport, while Steff was fit enough to use her new bike to commute, we agreed to buy a more reliable car with some of her accident compensation money. A while back we had bought a tatty old

Triumph Spitfire from Banksy. It had been great fun but needed constant attention, so we bought a characterful little Renault 4 instead. We needed to move the Spitfire on and the other mechanic, The Mumbler, was interested. He had a Suzuki GT500 so we agreed a straight swap. I didn't really want the bike, but it would take up a lot less room in the garage and it would be easier for me to sell on. Here it got complicated though as a friend of Allen's saw the Suzuki and took a liking to it. He had a nice but problematic 600cc Norton 99 Dominator twin, so wondered if I would consider a swap.

The Norton had a harsh engine knock, but I thought that if no additional money was involved it might be a decent deal, so I became a Norton owner. On taking the cylinder-head off, the valve-gear, pistons and cylinder bores were all in very good condition and there seemed to be no play in the conrods. I didn't think that the noise sounded like main bearings though and having eliminated most other possibilities, I removed the timing cover to discover that the cam sprocket was loose on the shaft. It can often be little things which cause the biggest problems.

A woodruff key had broken, so I rode down to Norton specialists, Fair Spares in Staffordshire to buy a new key and gaskets. I remember that ride fondly as it was probably the first proper one on the new Suzuki and made me realise that a big bike was pretty pointless for most needs; a good middleweight did everything that I needed from a motorbike. To cut a long story short the Norton's engine was mechanically super-quiet after that. I didn't really warm to it however, which wasn't helped by the top yoke coming off while I was riding it, resulting in a nasty fall. The wideline frame didn't suit my short legs either, I struggled to touch the floor, so I sold it. I mention this story primarily however as it was probably the only time that I have ever made a profit on a sale, the funds helping to pay for the little Renault 4, which was the whole purpose of selling the Spitfire in the first place.

Allen Steele had been busy over the winter, not with buying and preparing a new outfit but with finding a passenger: things had become messy. Tony had become *friendly* with Miss Castletown at the

Southern 100 prize-giving and had decided to leave his wife: his wife was Allen's sister! As such Tony had moved to the Isle of Man which was a double blow for Allen. He found that local passenger Colin Bairnson was available and enthusiastic however, so a new outfit paint scheme was adopted to commemorate the change even, in my opinion, if it didn't look as good as *our* previous speed-block livery.

Allen and Colin got used to each other during the early season meetings and managed a few leader board finishes. The TT was still the main focus however, even if it got off to a bad start. For the final practice session, Allen had fitted new pistons and rings and had decided to do a steady lap in order to run them in for the race. But even before he reached Ballacraine, going gingerly, a conrod broke, wrecking the crankcases. Back at the garage, Allen thought that his TT was over, when Ron Haslam's sponsor, the infamous hard man Mal Carter came over, *'What's the problem then?'* On seeing the extent of the damage he called over to Ron Haslam and simply told him to get his mechanics to bring his spare TZ750 engine and help Allen to fit it. Mal just asked Allen to let him have the engine back when he could afford to repair his own. It was incredible generosity from a larger than life character who didn't always get the best press.

Steff and I had gone to the Island, to our usual digs, on two bikes for the first time. We were both on our Suzuki twins, while Colin from work came down from where he was staying for an evening as he was over for the races too. He was on his new, well new to him, Ducati GT750, on which he had modified the silencers and the bike was ..... loud! In terms of the racing Mick Grant on the works Honda had a race-long battle with Suzuki's Graeme Crosby in the Formula I race. They exchanged the lead several times, with Grant eventually winning by eleven seconds. Irishman Sam McClements was third on a Honda. In the first Sidecar race, Allen and Colin retired due to fuel starvation unfortunately, with Trevor Ireson and Clive Pollington coming home six seconds in front of Jock Taylor and Benga Johannson. Dick Greasley and John Parkins were third. Allen found some problems with the fuel tank so had some repairs done between races and while they started the second race well, they were still troubled by a misfire.

It was due to foreign bodies in the fuel tank, presumably left after welding, which had made their way into the fuel. Allen had sensibly fitted a fuel filter, so stopped to unblock it and, despite the delay, the pair still got a fifteenth place finish, at an average of 92mph. The overall race result was a reversal of the first, with Taylor ahead of Ireson this time, Nigel Rollason and Dave Homer taking third on the Barton Phoenix. It was a huge anticlimax, so the highlight for us was Charlie Williams winning two races in one day; first the Formula Two which he led from start to finish and then the Junior race, in which he repeated the feat. It didn't quite make up for the disappointment of the sidecar events however and in the Southern 100 races Allen had problems again. In qualifying he managed to limp home in fifteenth and while he made the final, he suffered the only ever retirement of his Southern 100 career: of all things a spark plug broke.

Not long after returning from the Island Allen announced that he would be retiring at the end of the season. The costs involved in racing at National level were crippling and, despite a certain amount of sponsorship, he could no longer afford to compete. Although I wasn't

Allen and Colin at the TT in 1980. For Allen it was the end of the road and for all of us connected to his racing it came as a huge blow

really surprised, I was devastated; for the last five years going racing with Allen had consumed so much of my leisure time. It had provided so much excitement on what looked like Allen's trajectory to the big time. It was money alone which had stopped that. He had the talent, with World Champion Jock Taylor providing a fitting epitaph. At the last race of the season, at Oulton Park, Allen passed Jock at Old Hall corner. The wily Scot managed to re-pass, but Allen out braked him into Lodge at the end of the lap, overtaking him once again. Eventually, Jock used the superior speed of his Grand Prix engine to gain the lead, but at the end of the race, Jock stopped in the middle of the paddock and ran over to Allen, *'Why are you giving up? I gave it my best shot there and you still passed me, twice!'*

Irrespective, Allen retired from racing and all our lives were the worse for it. I continued to go to meetings, as there were still local riders I knew. Many were involved with the shop, but it just wasn't the same without being directly involved. I visited Allen at the house he now lived in at Great Barrow near Chester and of course we reminisced about our experiences. But gradually, my visits became less frequent and eventually I lost touch. Allen without racing wasn't the same man that I knew. Racing gave him his spark so his retirement was almost a bereavement for me. Life had to go on however and there were big things in the offing.

Finally, the time arrived for the new Wallasey branch of Tom Loughridge Motorcycles to open. Initially, I was there on my own and the first week or so was actually pretty boring. Gradually, I started to sell bikes however and I was soon up to about five or six a week. It was then that a major change of plan came about; the Sales Manager decided that *he* would like to run the new branch. So, I went back over to Heswall, to take over as Sales Manager there, and to be honest, I was more than happy with the arrangement. I had a shorter commute and it got me out of an uncomfortable relationship. At the new branch I would have always been under the existing Sales Manager to some extent. He would always be my first point of contact for bikes and spares, but now we'd have virtually no contact at all: perfect. Back in Heswall, the working atmosphere immediately improved; without exception, everyone was more relaxed. We felt more of a team and things got even better when Colin returned from his global travels as Workshop Foreman. The improved working atmosphere was really fortunate too, as it coincided with a very busy period. We were selling new bikes faster than we could un-crate them and I was going into work an hour early some days, just to build bikes up ready for sale. Throughout this period, I was working six days a week and loving every minute of it. Above all, we were in that happy situation where we all worked hard, but managed to have a great laugh at the same time. There were so many amusing incidents, and Colin was usually involved. One day he drove the Civic to Connah's Quay in North Wales to pick up some parts that we needed. About an hour later, the phone rang and I answered it to hear, *'The ****ing clutch has gone on the ****ing Civic! Get ****ing Old Tommy to come out in the van and we'll tow the ****ing Civic back'*

Now *'Old Tommy'* was a pleasant retiree who used to keep the bikes in the showroom polished. When I gave him the instructions as to where Colin and the stranded Honda were, I thought that he was going to have a heart attack. A twenty mile drive was obviously outside his comfort zone. I wasn't wrong. I later discovered that he owned a Volkswagen Beetle, bought brand new, and that after ten years of ownership it was still on its original tyres. None the less, Tommy was fully briefed. It took some time for him to take in the enormity of the task and he responded in his usual way when given any instruction with, *'What, now?'* Anyway, he reluctantly set off on what might have been his longest-ever journey.

About an hour and a half later, a white faced Tommy staggered into the workshop muttering, *'He's mad, he's mad!'* followed closely by Colin who was beside himself with laughter. Now, our ex-police V6 Ford Transit was a quick old device and Colin didn't drive it slowly. He had towed Tommy - who had probably never seen 50mph in his own car - back at over 70mph. At one point, on the dual carriageway, Colin had pulled out to overtake another vehicle and when he looked in the mirror Tommy was desperately still trying to stay in the inside lane! Tommy kept muttering and shaking his head for days after that

Throughout this period the rider training continued at a pace. Here I (left) have managed to rope in Charlie Williams (fifth right) to give some expert advice

incident, though it wasn't the only one in which the van was involved. On another occasion Colin decided to drive to Birkenhead at dinnertime to pick up some steel for a welding job on his Morris Minor. Out of boredom, the rest of us went with him, though as the transaction took longer than expected, it soon became apparent that we would probably be late back to the shop. This wouldn't have been a problem if Tom was around, but he wasn't, and I had visions of his wife - known to the staff as *'Mrs. Squiggly'* due to her terrible handwriting - opening the doors and trying to start selling. I had seen her in action before on the sales floor and the sales patter went something like this, *'Err, this is a nice blue one and err, this is a nice red one.'* It didn't bear thinking about, so Colin put his foot down and when we came to a long queue of traffic at a T-junction, all waiting to turn right, without a moment's hesitation Colin had the van on the pavement on the left. He passed everything and then, getting to the head of the line of traffic, he pulled out and turned right as well. At least I think that's what he did; I had my eyes shut for most of the time. Needless to say, we arrived back in time and Mrs. Squiggly was blissfully unaware that she had nearly been running the operation on her own.

Most of the humorous tales from Tom's involved Colin and a vehicle actually. Not long after the above story, Colin was again welding on his Morris Minor at dinnertime; those old rot-boxes were under constant repair. As he'd had a fire when welding in the past, he had taken the pin out of the workshop fire extinguisher as a precaution. Later, when we were all eating our dinner, Bill, the bike builder decided to have a cigarette. Being an ex-merchant seaman, he used to roll his own and, pausing to do this, he happened to lean on the extinguisher. It started to hiss and, quick as a flash, Colin shot across the workshop to give the valve a tap to re-seat it. Unfortunately, this only made matters worse, the hissing increased and soon a fine white powder engulfed the entire workshop.

Normally this wouldn't have been anything more than a minor inconvenience but, as it was a few days before the August registration of new bikes, the workshop was full of more than twenty brand new machines, now all covered with white powder. It took ages to get off, as if it was wiped it simply settled somewhere else: steam cleaning was required. Tom wasn't happy at all, and all that poor old Bill could say was, *'I've been set up!'* We had lots of fun, but it wasn't at the expense of doing any work. At the time we were managing to sell, service and repair *lots* of motorbikes. We were seeing record numbers, which strangely wasn't the case over at the other branch. Inexplicably sales at the new Wallasey shop began to drop off.

We were at a loss as to know why, when we were doing so well at Heswall, but before long I discovered the reason. A regular customer of mine was a merchant seaman who would buy a good second-hand bike every time that he was on leave, part exchanging his current machine as a trade in. One day he appeared at the shop asking if we had any BMWs. I told him that we had a nice one in stock at Wallasey and I could get it over for him to see. As it was a sunny day, he said, *'No problem'* and decided to ride over to look at it where it was. I thought no more about him until, two weeks later, he appeared on our forecourt on a Yamaha XS1100. I was surprised that he had bought a bike from somewhere else, as I knew that we didn't have one of the big Yamahas in stock. Trying not to sound annoyed, I casually asked where he'd bought the bike. He then told me that the Sales Manager at Wallasey put him off the BMW and sold him the Yamaha instead. Immediately, the alarm bells started ringing.

Of course, I told Tom and got the customer to repeat the conversation to him. The long and the short of it was that the Sales Manager had a stock of his own machines that he had been selling; no wonder he wanted to run a branch far away from us. This was why *'official'* sales were lower. Tom rang Wallasey and told him to shut the shop and come over. On the Sales Manager's arrival, he and Tom had a long meeting behind closed doors which resulted in the Sales Manager leaving. I returned to Wallasey for a short period until another salesman was employed, while understandably Tom was preoccupied for some time afterwards trying to work out how much the deception had cost. In the course of this I received several veiled threats from friends of the Sales Manager, but needless to say none of us ever saw him again and the threats never translated into anything physical. They didn't need to. I was put out of action by something else entirely. One morning I woke up to discover half my face was paralysed!

I remembered that when I was a kid, my mum had facial paralysis, which was diagnosed as Bell's Palsy. So, when I walked into the doctors the next morning, and he asked me - before even looking up from his previous patient's notes - what was wrong I gave my self-diagnosis, *'I think I've got Bell's Palsy'*. He immediately stared at my disfigured face and confirmed, *'I think you could be right.'* The doctor explained that the condition was caused by paralysis of a facial nerve and was usually temporary, but that the only treatment really was rest. He wrote out a sick note for a month and Tom took it brilliantly, reassuring me that I'd still be paid: what a great employer. I would spend much of my time sitting in the sunshine in the garden, feeling very bored and guilty until I hit on a way to pass the time. I had always loved looking at maps and I decided to plan a kind of navigation trial for my fellow instructors. I'd put together a list of about twelve locations in North Wales and the object of the trial would be to visit them all, in any order, covering the shortest possible distance. I fixed the points on the map and then, with Steff driving, I found the shortest routes. It was a nice diversion but thankfully within a month my face was more or less back to normal and I was relieved to be able to return to work. I think Tom put me on light duties however, as one of my first jobs was to drive the van down to Jack Lilley's dealership in Kent to collect a restored 1950s Moto Guzzi Falcone that Tom had bought for himself. The bright red 500cc flat-single was a beautiful machine, with its distinctive, massive, *'bacon slicer'* external flywheel and ultra-low tick-over. Tom never tired of demonstrating the latter to customers and, while I really fancied having a ride, it was the only bike Tom would never let anyone else on.

I was confined to my GSX400, and I used this to help me organise the navigation trial. The question was, would anybody want to take part? Luckily, when we assembled one sunny Sunday morning, about twelve riders turned up to have a go. I gave everyone a list of the checkpoints and told them that they could be visited in any order. Each rider had to make a note of their bike's odometer reading at the start, which I checked, so their total mileage could be calculated when they returned to the starting point. I gave them a cut-off time, when the rally would officially end, and to ensure that every rider visited all of the points I told entrants that three random points would be manned. These were looked after by Steff, myself and our friend Martin Tunnicliffe, Alex George's victim at Donington Park. My own checkpoint was at Ysbyty Ifan, in the heart of North Wales and I had a pleasant, peaceful day, that was occasionally interrupted by the sound of an approaching motorcycle. Thankfully, all the riders had been through by early afternoon, so I took a leisurely ride back to the start, where several riders had got within ten miles of my target distance. If I remember correctly a chap called Bob Hughes, on a Jawa won, with a mileage only four miles greater than mine. Everything had gone very well which, unfortunately, wasn't the same on the sales floor.

Almost imperceptibly, motorcycle sales started to slow down in the early eighties. My tests for the Observer had largely been of Superbikes but a large percentage of our shop sales were of ride-to-work machines. We sold new and second-hand Honda C50s, C70s, C90s and CG125s in huge numbers, largely as ride-to-work machines.

The pattern then was for families to have one car which the wife would use during the week to ferry the kids around, while the husband used his little bike to travel from home to work and back again. This began to change due to a number of factors. Some of the big local employers, Cammell Lairds shipbuilders being a prime example, began to make large scale redundancies, meaning that without work, the man of the house wouldn't be trading in his commuter bike every couple of years; he'd just be trading it in, full stop. Conversely, in families where both partners were working, owning two cars was increasingly becoming the norm; it was a viable and attractive option. Local redundancies also meant that for many motorcycling, as a leisure activity, was becoming unaffordable. As such sales of big bikes also slowed dramatically. We seemed to have more people trying to sell us bikes than enquiring about new ones. Checking with other dealers both locally and nationally revealed that we were not alone. The drop in demand was nationwide and while this didn't make us feel any better, at least we knew that we weren't doing anything wrong. We were probably doing better than most, but the future looked bleak. Reduced sales meant that the workshop was much quieter than normal, we were effectively overstaffed. The writing was on the wall and Colin gave in to his wanderlust and began planning a trip in his Land Rover to the Sahara Desert. His departure in a couple of months' time meant that no immediate redundancies were needed, but it was obvious that the Wallasey branch was no longer viable and a deal was done to sell it as a smaller operation, selling only spares and used machines.

When Colin said his farewells everyone's mood dropped. He was such a character and, irrespective of whatever might be going on, he always kept us laughing. He would be missed particularly as, while it was unspoken, there was little chance of him having a job to come back to on his return. For me, Colin's departure was eased somewhat by him leaving me his Ducati. He wanted it ridden regularly so my Sunday morning ritual from then on became an early start, kicking the 750 into life and quickly riding off before the resultant cacophony woke the neighbours. I would then head out for the Denbigh Moors, ride over them to the A5 and then back again before breakfast. The long-legged Ducati was made for the sweeping moorland roads. It would

Donington wasn't the only event I attended during this period. Life went on. This was a Chester MCC Grass Track race at Backford, as I always had my camera to hand

climb effortlessly, making a beautiful sound, as I revelled in the torque and handling. I still remember those fantastic rides, as Colin does; he still owns that amazing machine which, we discovered had an interesting history. One evening, Steff was looking through a pile of my Observer photos when suddenly she asked in a puzzled voice, *'What's a picture of Colin's Ducati doing in here?'* Convinced that she was confusing Colin's bike with the Mike Weston demonstrator that I road tested, I examined the picture, which *did* clearly show a very similar number plate. Still full of doubt, I went to the garage to double check the number on Colin's Ducati and, quite amazingly, it was the very same bike. I'd ridden Colin's bike a year or two before he had.

Those rides were important, as the outlook at work wasn't great. They picked me up, as did a trip as a guest to Tom, to a TT Riders' Association Annual Dinner. There were many great riders in attendance and I was lucky enough to sit next to Arthur Wheeler, pioneering Grand Prix rider and motorcycle dealer of note. Having ridden in the Grands Prix from 1949 until 1962, he entertained us with stories of his exploits around the circuits and came across as a real gentleman, as well as an obvious enthusiast. I also had the *honour* of standing next to John Surtees in the Gents, though I curbed my urge to talk to him as I feared distracting him from the job in hand!

Back at work Tom told me to sell my work bike as usual and in the spring he asked me to choose my machine for the following year. The only difference this time was that he asked me to choose something we already had in stock, as he was trying to keep down unnecessary expenditure. Knowing the worsening business situation, I chose a bike that the buying public had shown little interest in: a Suzuki GS550 Katana. The Katana series had been a bold styling exercise, a leap of faith by Suzuki, which they commissioned from the German stylists, Target Design. The 1000 and 1100 Katanas were truly ground-breaking, radical designs and were unsurprisingly really good sellers. The 650 and 550 however were rather watered-down versions of the concept, with only the tank and seat being different from the standard versions. They were something of a sheep in wolf's clothing, the 650 in particular with its heavy shaft final-drive. They were basically very sound bikes however and one benefit of the Katana over the standard model was the unusual, stepped, seat; it made for a very comfortable riding position. The GS550 was smooth, reasonably quick and ultra-reliable. It was also free so I couldn't complain, though later in the year, when a customer wanted to buy it, I sold without hesitation. As winter was approaching, Tom didn't want to register a new machine solely for my personal use, so I chose a second-hand MZ 250 Super Five this time, which we had taken in part-exchange. It had been owned by an enthusiast and had some worthwhile modifications. It had a Mikuni carburettor, was well sorted and was actually a real delight to ride. I didn't miss the Suzuki at all. I'm sure that others thought I was mad, but after bikes like the GS1000 the MZ made sense to me.

By the spring of 1983, prospects for the motorcycle trade really did look bleak. Sales had plummeted and I couldn't realistically see a future for me at Tom's, or indeed, anywhere else in the trade. I began to think of a career change and, as I'd enjoyed training people to ride motorbikes, I thought, *'How about being a teacher?'* As I had no 'A'

Levels, I didn't think that it was a realistic option, but I applied and to my surprise I was offered a place on a four year Bachelor of Education Honours degree programme. Best of all Tom was delighted for me. I was really concerned about how he'd take me letting him down and leaving, but he was actually struggling with how to break the same news to *me;* that he wanted to cut his losses and sell the business.

Before leaving Tom's we sold Steff's Suzuki GSX250 and bought a Honda CB250RS instead. I thought this would be cheaper to run and easier for me to service at home, and in many respects the RS250 exemplified everything that was going on in the market at the time. Honda offered two 250cc road bikes, the single-cylinder CB250RS and the Superdream twin. The Superdream was similar to the Suzuki GSX in many ways, and in comparison to the RS single it was slower, heavier, thirstier, handled worse and was more expensive. So – yeah you guessed it - they sold by the shed load, while RS singles stood riveted to showroom floors, gathering dust. No, I can't explain it either. For us the RS was ideal, a lovely little bike which was both practical and fun to ride. That Honda provided us with sterling service through my college years when money was tight and motorcycling in general, nationwide, seemed to be turning a corner.

Without putting an exact date on it, the start of the 1980s was, for me at least, the end of the *Golden Era.* I know that nothing stays the same, but at the time, so many things changed at once, both personally and professionally. I had finished working in the motorcycle trade, stopped writing my weekly column and, with Allen Steele's retirement, I lost direct involvement with motorcycle sport. On the roads the 125cc learner law came in, in February 1983, heralding the start of a long decline in road bike sales, which wasn't helped by ultra-fast and ultra-uncomfortable pseudo-race bikes rapidly taking over the big-bike market. The one constant was that I continued to act as Chief Instructor at Cheshire Motorcycle Training and that could have marked the end of my involvement in bikes, but for a chance encounter nearly fifteen years later.

Chapter 13
Never Say Never

C harlie Williams had long retired from racing by 1998. He had set up a shop in Chester however *'Everything but Bikes'*. In other words, a shop selling spares, clothing and accessories. On a visit back to Chester, and on a whim, I called in to ask if Charlie knew of Allen's whereabouts. I hadn't seen or heard of him in over a decade. Charlie was away at the time but Gary Dugdale, son of Hector Dugdale Junior, worked at the shop and he thought that Allen lived, *'Somewhere in Little Budworth'*, the village next to Oulton Park. Taking the bull by the horns I rode over, there and then thinking, *'It's a tiny village, everyone will know everyone else'*. I wasn't wrong. The third person I asked knew Allen and gave me directions to a detached house set in quite a large plot of land. There was a lady gardening near the front gate but before she could answer my question, as to whether Allen lived there or not, a familiar figure came strolling down the drive.

We were soon having a brew, catching up and talking about old times, and there must have been some serendipity as Allen had been wondering how to get in touch with *me*. He was starting to get involved with racing again. He had been approached by the organisers of the Manx Grand Prix, as the 1998 races were to be the 75th anniversary of the event and they were planning to have a past winners' parade. They had invited Allen, who had bought a Yamaha TZ250; this wasn't up and running yet, but another friend had filled the breach, offering a similar machine. I had to be there, so come the day I arrived at Ronaldsway airport, caught a bus into Douglas and found Allen in the paddock, behind the grandstand. The bike looked well, as did Allen in brand new leathers and we had a great catch up, talking about the old times at the TT with Nigel King among others, ex-works Yamaha mechanic to Charlie Williams. We were so involved in our chatter that we didn't realise that racing had been delayed and of course, once the implications of that gradually sunk in I realised that I would possibly miss the parade because of my fixed flight home. The inevitable happened, as while I caught some of the rescheduled racing from Quarter Bridge I wasn't able to wait for the parade. I was dejected, but shouldn't have been. I thought I'd missed the curtain going down, the last hurrah of an illustrious racing career; I hadn't, I'd actually witnessed the start of a second! By the following year Allen had finished his own TZ250 Yamaha and entered into a series called The TZ Challenge. The Challenge was a series at Cadwell Park, where each *race* was actually a type of time trial; the riders setting their own pace and then trying to lap at a consistent speed. It was a low-key, no pressure affair for Allen to get back into riding, though we were also tasked with keeping an eye on a novice rider called Rob Knight, whose dad had asked Allen for a helping hand. Incredibly I had never seen Allen on a solo, but I wasn't surprised it was like witnessing a duck to water. He looked like he had never been off one, winning the first event and eventually the whole series. In comparison, young Rob's initial rides on a Yamaha FZR600 were *steady*. I thought he'd struggle to be competitive, but Allen agreed to prepare his engines and soon more work came along.

Allen on his own Maxton, in 2000. Again back on the Island

The following season Allen also took on the task of getting a 400 version ready for the Manx Grand Prix, for a friend called Dave Brough. The 400 Yamaha was a good looking little bike with real potential and one of a number of odd-ball *'grey import'* 400cc, four-cylinder machines around on the track at the time. Most weren't officially imported into this country but they were very popular in the F3/Production class and Allen soon had this one flying. Obviously, Allen was planning to be at the Manx to look after the bike, but as he couldn't really afford to go for the whole fortnight, Rob Knight and myself agreed to go over too. The bombshell, once we arrived, was that Dave had failed to qualify, though there was a silver lining. For the first time in twenty years I had a bike on the Island. I'd ridden over and after Rob had taken my Suzuki SV650 out for a lap he came back smiling, *'I'm going to race the Manx one day!'* Pipe dreams, I thought.

It was around this time that Allen and I had our memorable trip to the Ulster Grand Prix which I mentioned at the beginning of the story. What really made that trip was the absolute dedication to motorcycle road racing that we encountered, alongside the legendary Northern Irish hospitality. The place was buzzing and it was obvious that the Ulster was at least as important to people in Northern Ireland as the FA Cup Final is over here, on the mainland. The real eye-opener was when well-known sponsor Billy McKinstry drove us around Lisburn where he lived, introducing us to a number of people who, despite having very run-of-the-mill jobs, somehow managed to sponsor motorbike racers. We visited several unimposing, semi-detached houses and headed with their respective owners straight to regulation suburban up-and-over garages, where one or more - often quite remarkable - race bikes lived. The icing on the cake was when we were heading back to Billy's house. We drove past a little old lady who was trudging back from the shops. She was heavily laden with plastic bags full of her purchases and we would never have even noticed her if it wasn't for Billy pointing her out, *'See her there? She sponsors so and so on an RG500, he'll be out on it tomorrow!'* For the life of me and to my shame, I can't remember either the lady's or the rider's name, but I think you get the picture. I thought, *'If only the mainland could be like this?'*

It was a bit more mundane on my side of the water, where the following season Allen rode in a few club races on his 250 Yamaha. Despite being in his sixties, he was still competitive and Rob Knight, now riding a Honda RS125, entered the same events. At one Cadwell meeting however, Allen had a low-speed tumble. Half in jest I told him that he was too old for solos, 'You should get a sidecar again'. It wasn't a serious suggestion, it was more just to gee him on, as I thought he might pack it in. How wrong could I be?

You guessed it; one day, in early July 2001, I got an excited phone call, directly to my office in school, 'John, I need a sponsor; I've bought an outfit!' A mutual friend, who raced a Yamaha TZ350-powered sidecar, had seen a similar one for sale, for £1,400, and he had given Allen the contact information. When Allen had introduced himself, the seller, a chap called John Phillips, had asked, 'Not the Allen Steele who raced outfits in the 70s?' as it turned out that they had raced and knew each other from those days. After reminiscing for a while, Allen said, 'If the outfit sits more or less straight and has three wheels, I'll have it.' Well, it was a much better deal than that.

Allen's call to me was, I suppose, in the hope that I might chip in with a couple of hundred pounds, but after talking to Steff that night, I phoned him with an offer that he couldn't refuse: we'd go the whole hog. Steff and I would sponsor him to the tune of £700, plus an interest-free loan for the other £700, for as long as it was needed. There was a condition however, 'Allen, the outfit has to have the same black, red and white, 1978, speed-block colour scheme.' I don't think that either of us could take in what was happening, certainly not me, but when Allen had stopped racing in the early 1980s it left a huge hole in my life. I became depressed about my lack of involvement. Honestly, I used to dream that Allen had started racing again and now he really was.

The very next Saturday Allen, Rob Knight and myself headed to Derby and when we met John Phillips, both Allen and myself recognised him straight away. We spent a few minutes talking about the old days and as we were chatting, John pulled the cover off one of several outfits in his garage. It was beautiful, pristine, so Allen asked, 'So, OK, where's *the one that's for sale?'* John replied, *'You're looking at it'.* We couldn't believe what great condition it was in. It was straight and level, looking as if it was ready to race. The only downside was that it was fitted with a road-going LC350 engine, but Allen already had an answer to that. He had his Maxton race bike at home, with a TZ350 engine in it that would fit.

The sidecar chassis was built by John Derbyshire, a well-respected constructor, and one thing that we knew for sure was that we'd got ourselves an absolute bargain. When we got it back to Allen's, we poked and prodded at it, but could find very little wrong and within a few days Allen phoned me to say that the TZ engine was now in. The outfit was a runner and the engine would burst into life after just three steps. Things were looking good, particularly as Allen had found a passenger. His partner Mags had a nephew called Jim Edwards who was keen to have a go and he had all the right credentials. He had the right build, was fit and strong and was mad. The latter went without saying, as they had already entered the outfit for a race meeting at Ty Croes, on Anglesey, before Jim had even applied for his licence.

Allen and Jim had a few shakedown rides and were ready for the British F350 (Formula 350) Championship the following spring. This series had grown out of the F2 (Formula Two) Championship, which had been specifically set up to counter the rising costs of sidecar racing. As we knew to our cost, running a TZ750 powered outfit was prohibitively expensive, so a series catering for 350cc machines, pretty much all of them TZ350s, was seen as the way forward. It was hugely successful, but as two-strokes fell out of favour on the road the F2s moved to a mixed 350cc two-stroke/600cc four-stroke formula. The majority of machines are 600cc today, but at the time, as the change-over took place, this left a huge number of highly developed 350cc outfits with pretty much no place to call home. As such the F350 British Championship was created and this was the series in which Allen and Jim planned to compete. How competitive they would be remained open to question, but before the first meeting of the season I discovered I was also to ride a race bike again. It would be the first time in nearly forty years and it came care of another Allen Steele

Allen and Jim on the F350 outfit. I imagine people thought that Allen was an old has-been, reliving his youth, but they were soon at the heart of the action

phone call, *'You know there's a meeting at Oulton Park next month? Well, I've got you a ride on my TZ250!'* Here we go again, I thought, *'Blimey, OK Allen!'*

We both knew that I'd neither got a race licence nor the time to obtain one, so what was going on? Well, Derek Huxley was another top local solo rider, a contemporary of Charlie Williams and Stan Woods. He was organising a Past Masters parade and, for some reason best known to him, Allen had asked Derek if I could be added to the list. It was stupid – I was a *'Past Amateur'* - but Derek agreed and a few weeks later there I was, terrified, lined-up at Oulton Park, on a cold spring morning on a bike that I had never ridden before. My mood wasn't helped when Bill Smith wandered over to offer me some sage words of advice, *'The track's slippery, you need to take it steady lad or you'll soon be off.'* That really boosted my confidence, particularly as the heavens opened as they let us out onto the grid where I managed at least to

The author and TZ250. I'll be honest, it wasn't a marriage made in heaven

shuffle myself to the back; I wanted to keep out of the way of those who knew what they were doing. The flag dropped and, fearful of stalling the engine, I screamed the little Yamaha away from the line. Following the huge cloud of spray created by the riders in front, I did my best, I really did, but oh, was the power-band vicious. Until the revs were somewhere in the red, nothing much happened at all then, suddenly, all hell let loose. Just what you want in the wet! As I came over Hilltop the thing was accelerating so quickly that I'd hardly changed into one gear when the engine was red-lining and needed the next. Thankfully I didn't have to concern myself with the handling, it was superb. I had no trouble putting the bike where it was meant to be on the track, which is more than could be said for Bill Smith. As I dropped down to Knickerbrook, there he was, sitting on the straw bales next to the bike that he had just fallen off. *'Do as I say, not as I do'* sprung to mind.

I was still on the bike but feeling pretty flat in the conditions so eventually came into the pits. I was worried I'd be lapped and felt I hadn't done the bike justice, when Charlie Williams came over and asked, *'What did you come in for? You were going really well, starting to catch a few.'* I don't know if Charlie said it just to make me feel better, probably, but if so it certainly did the trick. The experience still only reinforced my existing opinion however; racing just isn't for me. I still have a copy of the programme though, even if I feel such a fraud when I read my name under the *'Past Masters Challenge'* alongside Phil Read, Bill Smith, Terry Grotefield, Tommy Robb and the rest. Soon after, in a local pub, I got talking to BBC Radio DJ Andy Kershaw. I knew that he was an enthusiast and had written an article about a similar ride that he had on a TZ250. On comparing notes our thoughts were very similar; to ride those bikes properly required a good deal more bottle and far greater talent than ours. These guys were real stars, though that sheen didn't always extend beyond the track.

For the life of me, I can't remember if this event was before or after my Oulton outing, but one day around the same time, Allen rang me up sounding unusually flustered. It turned out that Bill Smith had asked him if he had a spare bike for another parade and, assuming that Bill wanted to ride, Allen offered his 350 Spondon. Bill thanked him, then casually added, *'It's for Phil Read to ride.'* Now, without going into details, Phil Read - fantastic rider that he was - was known in racing circles as someone *not* to lend a bike to. I prefer not to put names in print, but a number of people had loaned him bikes and later wished that they hadn't; let's just leave it at that.

As such Allen was in a quandary; having promised the bike, he didn't want to let Bill Smith down, but neither could he afford to get himself embroiled in some post-parade financial or liability issue. I told Allen, *'Leave it with me. I'll think of something.'* And this is what I thought. On arrival at the circuit, we took the bike over to Phil Read. Allen was pushing it and I approached Phil armed with a little duplicate book. I proffered it to the superstar and, thinking that I just wanted an autograph, he was about to sign it when I said, *'You better read it first.'*

Phil looked puzzled and, as he read the following, a frown appeared on his face.

I, Phil Read agree to loan Allen Steele's 350cc Spondon Yamaha subject to the following conditions;

1. If I crash the machine, I will recompense Allen Steele in full for repairs.
2. I will not expect any financial recompense as a result of this loan.
Signed: ……………. Phil Read

After reading this, an obviously annoyed Mr. Read said, *'I'm not signing that!'* as I strategically placed myself between the Yamaha and Phil. I was not moving either, *'No signature, no bike'* and, realising that he was between a rock and a hard place, he countered with, *'What if it seizes?'* Once I had reassured him that we would not expect him to pay for engine failures, he reluctantly signed and agreed. Walking back to our van both Allen and I were grinning; there was no way that bike was going to seize. It was over-geared and the carburettors were jetted heavily on the rich side. So, give the multiple Word Champion his due, despite the way that Allen had set the bike up, he was easily as fast as circuit specialist Charlie Williams in the *Parade*! Returning the Yamaha to us afterwards, Phil was very complimentary about it and he gave Allen a signed photo of himself. Myself? I just got a wary look, a grunt and wide berth.

At our age parading of course was the appropriate thing to be doing, but as the 2002 race season started things for the team actually went up a gear. I say *team* as somehow we were now running one, with Rob Knight joined by Mikey Edwards on Honda RS125s. We were known as BSK Racing, with the letters standing for the initials of our original supporters. As the personnel changed over the years, so did the meaning, though we settled for *'Bikes Since Kids'*. It summed us up pretty accurately and in 2002 BSK's year was most notable for the up-coming Manx Grand Prix. When Rob had ridden my Suzuki around the Island and told me that he would like to ride in the Manx, I thought that it was just wishful thinking. I hadn't realised how determined he was and, since getting his Honda RS125, Rob's riding had come on in leaps and bounds. He was becoming competitive at National level and when he announced that his entry for the Manx Newcomer's race had been accepted he asked Allen and myself to be his pit crew. We were off to the Island again.

On Thursday 15th August I left home on my current bike, a Honda Transalp, but only as far as Allen's. He'd bought a 7½ tonne Ford Cargo lorry that had been converted into a proper race transporter; things were getting serious. It had a bedroom/kitchen behind the cab and plenty of space for bikes in the back. As such, we loaded my bike in the back for the crossing, as this was to be our home for the next fortnight, when we set up in the paddock alongside Rob's van. We were all far too excited to sleep on the ferry over to Douglas, and on arrival Rob soon set off on my Transalp for a couple of laps. Once he returned and as it was such a lovely evening, I did a lap too and I couldn't help but notice how much smoother a number of sections of the course were now; though in fairness my first visit was over forty years before.

Rob Knight was a different rider once on the two-stroke Honda RS125. A perfect match

The next day Rob went for the compulsory Newcomers lap of the course, in a coach, before his first practice session, for which I took Mikey on the back of my Honda, to watch from Quarter Bridge. Rob's RS sounded really crisp as he went through, accelerating off towards Braddan Bridge, after which the Classics were next past, it being great to hear the sound of big singles on the Island again. I had expected Rob to arrive back with us at Quarter Bridge after about thirty-five minutes, so I was pleasantly surprised when he turned up just twenty-nine minutes after leaving us. I was even more impressed when Rob later told me that the visibility was so poor over the Mountain that he'd been in first gear for some of the time.

After a successful and trouble-free start to the event, we were all in high spirits. We piled into the van to drive to Ramsey for a Chinese meal, after which we continued round the circuit to help with Rob's familiarisation. With Rob driving, we set off up May Hill towards Ramsey Hairpin, but climbing up out of the Gooseneck, Allen announced that he should have gone to the toilet before we left. Needless to say having stopped, we then pulled away again, Allen shouting, *'You b***ards!'* behind us. We were glad we didn't leave him for good however as his knowledge was to prove priceless. The higher that we got, the lower the Manx mist came down. The visibility was really poor and yard-by-yard, Allen guided Rob down the Mountain, telling him when to keep to the centre of the road and when to turn in for each corner, even though the rest of us couldn't see the corners at all. It was massively impressive, we hadn't got a clue, but perhaps it rubbed off as in Monday's practice Rob really flew.

Allen told Rob that when he won the Manx in 1970 he had ridden a lap on a road bike before every session, so that he knew what the conditions were like before every practice and race. It was sound advice and Rob set off on my Transalp, in the dark, lapping in under forty minutes. For the actual session, I took Mikey up to watch from Creg ny Baa, where Rob knocked fourteen minutes off those forty. He lapped in around twenty-six minutes. For the next session I went to the Crosby Hotel where Mikey was amazed at the speed of the bikes as they screamed passed us, just feet from the pub wall. Rob looked to be going even better this time, clocking an average speed of 88mph, easily qualifying for the race. One of our paddock neighbours, John McDean, had been less fortunate. His Classic 250 Suzuki had stopped and, from the sound of it, needed an engine strip which involved – as is so often the case in the paddock – everyone round about getting somehow sucked in. John stripped his Suzuki engine and, finding that it had run a big-end bearing phoned our friend Derek Huxley in Ellesmere Port, in order to organise a crank rebuild. It was decided a sidecar racing friend, Paul Lightfoot, who by chance was helping John, would fly back to the mainland to get the crankshaft rebuilt by Derek and then fly back with it again. In the meantime John would try to cobble something together. As is the way of these things, it was all a bit hectic.

On the Wednesday morning, I was wandering through the paddock when I met Chester rider Pat Wynne, who was over to ride his Classic Ducati single. Pat asked me who I was with and what I was doing, and enquired if I would have any free time. To cut a long story short I got roped in to being a marshal, as Pat knew I'd done the same on the mainland. I was asked where I'd like to be stationed and which sessions, and opted for Hillberry, where I was told to report to the Sector Marshal. Mikey came with me, but this time not on the pillion. Welsh rider, Gordon Powell, had a spare Cagiva 125 road bike with him, of which he said Mikey could have a loan. Gordon didn't know that Mikey was underage and, for some reason, it never occurred to us to tell him!

At Hillberry I met a couple with their daughter who had marshalled at this point for many years. Robin and Annette Daykin and their delightfully named daughter, Tree, were to become good friends over the years and would come to write their own chapter in TT history. I had chosen Hillberry chiefly however as I knew that it was a corner that would sort the men out from the boys. A fast, downhill right-hander under some trees, Allen said that he could take it flat out on his 250 in the 1970 Manx. I was to see many riders drop one, or even two gears here however, with the difference between riders in the same class being as much as 20mph. My main interest was watching Rob though and while by no means the fastest, Rob was quicker than many and he improved his time, lapping at 91mph.

Happy with the day, we headed out for some food. The previous evening, we'd arrived back too late in town to eat at The Ranch restaurant in Douglas, but tonight was to be different. The staff had promised to keep a table for us, though ultimately it only helped add to Mikey's list of driving offences. After the meal a waitress told us not to rush off; they were having a staff party and we were invited for a lock-in. We didn't take much persuading. The drink flowed freely and when eventually - and much the worse for wear - we staggered out to the van we realised that we were all far too drunk, apart from Mikey. Quick-thinking Allen had the solution, young Mikey would have to drive. Allen's logic was impeccable. Mikey was the only sober one amongst us, so he couldn't be accused of drunk driving. The fact that he was several years off being able to even apply for a provisional licence didn't seem to be a consideration for the assembled party of drunks and, to be fair, Mikey drove us very steadily back to base. He panicked a little when he saw a police car in his mirror, but Allen just told him to drive normally

The Manx 2002 dream team. (L to R) Myself, Paul Dumbill a racing friend of Allen's from way back, Allen himself and Rob Knight

and, thankfully, the policeman didn't notice the remarkably youthful driver at the wheel. Were we irresponsible? Probably. Does Mikey still have fond memories? Definitely.

The Friday was a busy one. Allen was up before any of us at 7.00am so that he could fit a new piston to Rob's bike without any interruptions. I invited my fellow marshals, the Daykin family, to come to see us in the paddock and they were quite overwhelmed. In all their years of marshalling, no one had ever invited them to the paddock, so I was really pleased. Despite being busy, our team made them very welcome. I don't know if this was a factor or not but as a footnote dad, Robin Daykin, later talked about racing an old Royal Enfield outfit that he had bought. I must admit that I thought that it sounded a bit pie in the sky, but I hadn't taken in Robin's single-mindedness. Before long, he was campaigning it all over Europe, with Annette in the chair, and eventually they bought a modern Yamaha outfit which, to complete their dreams, they raced as *'Team Past it'* at the Isle of Man TT.

That sort of thing takes grit, the very sort which John McDean was demonstrating next to us back in 2002. He temporarily rebuilt his 250 Suzuki using an old spare crank, whilst Paul Lightfoot was away getting his race crank sorted. John didn't trust the bodged version to last race distance, but he thought that he might be able to complete the critical qualifying lap. With no Paul to assist him, John was up against it and as such I helped by taking his bike through scrutineering. Alas it was to no avail as, despite all of his efforts, the bike stopped on the Cronk y Voddy straight. John only had one session left in which to qualify, though he put a brave face on. Rob in comparison did just one steady lap, to scrub in his new tyres on his RS125, and bed in the new piston and rings. He still lapped at 80mph though, which was really pretty fast. The following morning I drove John's van down to Ronaldsway airport, whilst he stripped his Suzuki engine in the paddock. I collected Paul from the airport and, as soon as we were back in Douglas, he and John rebuilt and fitted the motor. John got out for the final session and managed to qualify for the race. After all of his trials and tribulations he deserved it, we'd all put in a shift.

Saturday, we were up early, in order to prepare Rob's pit. Allen was on refuelling and Paul, another friend, on generally checking the bike over. I was assigned visor cleaning and on giving Rob a drink, and both Paul and I were designated pushers, to get Rob going again afterwards, which completed the pit stop. We went down to the pit in our normal clothes to practice, until a jobsworth from the ACU came to throw us out: we weren't in our fireproof overalls. *'Is that ACU blazer that you're wearing fireproof?'* Allen asked. The official was lost for an answer, but we trudged back anyway to collect our *'uniforms'* as it wasn't worth arguing the toss. There was actually little room in the pit, so we rehearsed how we would manage, without getting in each other's way. With years of experience, Allen also had a trick up his sleeve that would ensure our refuelling was quicker than others. It wasn't a cheat but, looking around at other crews, it didn't seem to be something that they were aware of: Allen over-filled the gravity fuel dump. This meant that there was a much greater weight of fuel, so the bike's tank filled up faster than the others. Allen added two extra gallons, that would do the trick.

Before the race Rob was understandably nervous, but he set off well and the three of us in the pits then anxiously waited, watching the huge scoreboard opposite us. It had a set of lights for each rider - at least it did back then - which would light up in turn as the rider passed each section of the course. We were watching the light which would show us that Rob had reached Glen Helen, but although those of riders with similar start numbers illuminated, Rob's didn't. We knew that the system wasn't foolproof however, so we didn't panic and after what seemed an age, Rob's light for Signpost finally lit up and within no time at all, he was back with us.

The stop ran like clockwork; so well in fact that poor Rob was still trying to ask us how he was doing as Paul and I were pushing him away from the pit. It was one of the quickest pit-stops of the race so we kept our fingers crossed. We needn't have worried. Rob finished a very creditable fifth with an average speed for the race of over 92mph. It had been a great result, so could 2003 deliver any better?

Chapter 14
Groundhog Day

Well, for me, 2003 was in so many ways a case of déjà vu. On the negative side - and contradicting what I'd previously said about myself and race tracks - I had another ride out on a race machine. Jerry Lodge is a partner in Earnshaw's Motorcycles, in Huddersfield, and has a bevy of beautiful little Honda MT125 machines. I was asked if I'd like to ride one and so, with my younger - but also bike mad - brother Phil, I headed for Anglesey with the little racer on the trailer. Unfortunately, just before the parade started, I discovered several broken spokes in the rear wheel. I was in a quandary as to whether to go onto the circuit or not, but decided to ride and it was a big mistake. Due to the state of the wheel I had no confidence at all and in short, I was soon getting in the way of faster riders. I came into the paddock with my tail well and truly between my legs. I'd discovered again that you should never venture onto a race circuit on an unfamiliar bike: I could have lapped faster on my Transalp. The story behind the ride was the key thing however.

For many years, I had been buying bikes from Earnshaw's in Huddersfield. I had developed a good relationship with the owners, the Lodge brothers, Jerry, Jason and Jamie, and I had of course told them about my time in the motorcycle trade. As a result, one day totally out of the blue, Jerry asked me if I would like to work for them, at the weekends, as a salesman. I dismissed the idea out of hand when I thought about how busy I was teaching, but in truth I was tempted, *'I'll do it'*. We negotiated hours that were agreeable to both and it was all agreed very quickly, as the very next Saturday I started work, back on the sales floor, after a gap of over twenty years. Blimey! I was genuinely surprised at how naturally I fell back into the role and perhaps unsurprisingly it didn't feel like work at all; more like a hobby, just standing around, talking about bikes and getting paid for the privilege as well. I was soon selling quite a few bikes and Earnshaw's were as pleased as me. There were other perks to the job: I got a good discount on parts, clothing and accessories and I also had the option of buying any bikes that I took in part-exchange. One I turned down I still regret to this day: a Laverda 750SF similar to the one owned by Tom Loughridge. It was in good condition, the price was right but, for some reason, I turned the offer down. What a prize idiot. Another similar case was a very nice example of Moto Guzzi's little shaft-drive 500cc V-twin, the V50. That was another regret at Earnshaw's, though everything else at the shop continued really well for quite some time. Until, as often happens, along comes something to turn it upside down. The *thing* in this case was the appointment of a full-time sales-man. He was a nice enough bloke, but his style was totally different to mine. When a potential customer came into the showroom I would give them time to look around, noticing if they gravitated towards a particular model or type of machine. I'd approach and engage them in conversation about the bike and how it might suit their needs. The method was largely successful, as I never put any pressure on a customer to buy. Our new salesman's style was totally different. Hardly had a customer got through the door before he'd be on them. Within seconds he would have them standing by the bike that *he* thought they needed - or the shop needed to sell - extolling its virtues until he had them like a fly in a spider's web. Many of them, particularly the young and inexperienced, ended up buying bikes whether they were the ones that they really wanted or not. Perhaps this was what Earnshaw's wanted? Maybe I was wrong but I wasn't comfortable with the way things were going and, anyway, there wasn't really room for both of us working on the same sales floor. I left on good terms, continuing to buy bikes from Earnshaw's, so I was mildly amused to see that the high pressure salesman didn't last long.

I'd actually told the shop that my main reason for leaving was the pressures of my teaching job. It was true, but there was actually a lot more going on, much of it fuelling that feeling of déjà vu. Around the turn of the decade there seemed a lot mirroring the 1970s. It got me thinking about writing again and I fancied a bit of a challenge. I remember yelling to Steff; *'I think I'm going to try journalism again!'* I can't recollect what her reaction was, but I still read the monthly magazines, UBG - Used Bike Guide – in particular and thought I could write as well. UBG featured reviews of current or recent models every month, written by actual owners. At the time it was a new angle and the publishers paid for anything that they printed, unlike the case with readers' contributions today. I was intrigued, so thought, *'What have I got to lose?'*

In truth I was mainly interested in whether a national magazine would still consider my work, particularly as the general style of writing had changed a lot. The subject matter however was easy; an extended road test and appraisal of the two Honda Transalps I'd owned, as out of habit I had plenty of pictures. I had covered thousands of miles on the Hondas, I doubt anyone knew them as well and I ended up with quite a lengthy article. Editing was never my strong point, but my thinking was that it was better to write too much and allow the editor to cut it, than to write too little and have it consigned to the bin – though as a word of advice, editors generally like stuff to be of a perfect, given, word count, it makes everyone's life easier that way.

I sent the article off and then waited. As usual, I bought the magazine, but as the months passed without me hearing anything, I thought, *'Ah well, perhaps I simply haven't got it anymore?'* The truth is that magazines don't work like daily or weekly papers. They have layouts planned, often many issues in advance, so freelancers' articles are slotted in as and when space allows. As such, in March 2004, I was studying the front cover of the April issue of UBG in WH Smith's, when I noticed some small print at the foot of the page. Sandwiched between *'Supercharged 600 Bandit'* and *'Chris Walker's Fantasy Garage'* were two words that put a smile on my face. How sad was that? *'Honda Transalp'!* For a moment I thought how awful I'd feel if it was written by someone else. But before I had chance to dwell on the unthinkable, the following jumped off the page;

> *'Page 41 Honda Transalp X 2. John Moulton replaced the bike he bought, his Transalp, with………….. another Transalp. Say no more.'*

There, under the headline *'Big Softie'* was my article covering five pages complete with photos. Not a single word had been cut and within a couple of days I received several copies of the magazine through the post from editor, Brian Tarbox, along with an accompanying letter. He'd enjoyed my writing, *'Would you consider submitting more?'* Best of all was the enclosed cheque. An article on touring Southern Ireland followed and over the next few years I became a regular contributor. I established a good rapport with Brian and would probably still be writing today were it not for a change of editor. It was good while it lasted however. It enabled me to relive my 1970s writing days, while I was still involved in present day racing which in 2003 was going very well.

Rob Knight entered the Ultra-Lightweight race at the Manx again, but as this class also now catered for 400cc four-strokes, he was just looking to be competitive against the other 125s and hoping for a finish in the top ten. It was much the same set up as the year previously but Jim, Allen's passenger, was with us this time. I took him to the Crosby Hotel to watch his first ever practice session. He'd never even been to the Island before so, as expected, the speed of the bikes passing inches away blew him away. Rob looked very comfortable on his RS125 from the same viewing spot, lapping at about 94mph, but what I remember most was a big trail bike, a Honda 1000cc Varadero, circulating very neatly, very quickly. I regret not looking up who it was, but I had a lot on at the time. I was picking up my brother David from the boat as I had persuaded him to come over for the first time in about thirty years and, after dropping his gear in the paddock, all of us went down to Castletown to see Adjers, Allen's passenger from the 1970s. Adjers and Allen had been really close and we reminisced about their TT and Southern 100 successes. I reminded Allen about Adjers waving to the nurses when they were racing at New Brighton in their first season on the BSA, while Allen told me a couple of tales about Adjers and the ladies, which I can't possibly recount here.

It all brought back memories of their Yamaha outfit screaming past the grandstand towards Bray Hill in 1978, but in 2003 it was Hillberry from where I watched the Newcomers and Classic Senior races. The Classic was won by Bill Swallow and, regardless of capacity or age of machine ridden, Bill was one of the fastest through Hillberry all week, showing the riders of many modern machines how to do it. This was the sort of knowledge that would have been useful the following day, as myself, Allen and Rob were at the ferry terminal to pick up a young racer who was coming over for the very first time. We'd met this young, bike-mad girl when she started to race at Oulton Park. I remember seeing her mum struggling to push a 125 Honda to scrutineering, so I offered to take over for her. We kept seeing this

Rob Knight and the BSK Racing RS125. Rob was really on it by 2003

mum and daughter at local meetings, gradually getting to know each other well. Anyway, back to the Island, when we picked the mystery girl up, she asked if we could do a lap of the course so that she could see what all the fuss was about. Her name was Jenny Tinmouth and she's a TV pundit now. She holds the record for the fastest TT lap by a female competitor at 119.945mph and every time I see her I remind her of that very first lap, in our van. It was a nice interlude in a busy week, where I found time to watch a very fast and very smooth Jason Griffiths win the Junior Classic on a Honda 350 twin. It sounded beautiful and I was - and still am - amazed at how such an ordinary road bike like the Honda CB350K4 could be transformed into such a machine. The road version I tested in the 1970s was a pretty awful, pedestrian thing, so I doubt there was anything from Honda still in that astounding motor.

There was a practice session after that race and Rob completed a single lap. When he came in, he said that he wasn't happy with the bike's suspension, though we couldn't find anything amiss. We presumed that as Rob was riding progressively faster, he was simply exploring the limits of the machine. As we were puzzling about what, if anything, to do - especially as the race was on the next day - Rob got chatting to 125 TT winner Chris Palmer. Chris instantly offered to come and have a look at the bike and, in no time at all, he was making adjustments mirroring the settings on his own. The settings made the suspension much softer than Rob had been using, but with no further practice, we just had to trust Chris. He seemed a genuine, decent guy and we found our trust was well founded. Next day the tweaking had worked: Rob lapped at an unbelievable 97mph, his best time yet. The pit stop was quick and trouble free too and Rob finished third 125cc machine home: job done.

That wasn't it for 2003 however. After achieving eighth place competing in their first year of the F350 Championship, Allen and Jim were hoping for even better things. Most of the technical bugs had been ironed out and Allen and Jim were working much better together on the outfit. They rarely finished out of the top six and had a number of second and third places, usually behind eventual championship winner, John Crick. They won the final round of the FSRA F350 Championship however, the same round at which I had my ignominious MT125 ride, and the significance was that by winning the final round they secured second place in the championship. Everyone was delighted and shortly after I, Allen and Duncan, a retired policeman who had become an integral part of the team, travelled to Doncaster to look at a Windle 350 outfit. It was in excellent condition and, as it would be a significant step up from Allen and Jim's current outfit, Duncan dipped into his retirement funds to buy it. We were all amused by this as indirectly the police had bought us a new racing machine. Again, it was like the 1970s, when Allen moved from the BSA to the Weslake, Weslake to the Suzuki and then on once more.

Things didn't go quite to plan for BSK Racing in 2004, at least not to begin with. In TT practice Rob improved his fastest lap to 103mph – remember, on a 125cc – but for the first time ever and despite impeccable preparation, he broke down in the race. That's the TT all over, as on the mainland things went better. Charlie Williams agreed to sponsor BSK Racing for the season, as Charlie was and still is enormously grateful to Allen for the help he provided when Charlie was starting out. Allen was touched by the gesture and, unbeknown to him, Charlie and I had arranged a special presentation for him at Anglesey. The meeting marked exactly forty years since Allen had started racing, at Oulton Park in 1964, on his BSA C15, so a vague tannoy announcement called Allen to race control during a break in the racing. Thinking that he was in trouble, he went somewhat reluctantly, but arrived to find myself, Charlie and many other competitors gathered to see him awarded a special trophy, made by Charlie himself. For once in his life, Allen was speechless. I could go over the rest of the season, blow-by-blow, but suffice to say Allen and Jim had a great year. They won plenty of races and a second and a fourth place at Pembrey, at the last meeting of the year, meant that at nearly sixty five years old, Allen had won the FRSA F350 Sidecar Championship: some achievement.

2005 was a watershed, as having won the title Allen decided to take a back seat at BSK Racing, letting others take the strain. Cheshire driver

Mick Finnie and Joe Shardlow. Brief but much missed sparring partners, while Mick was still around

Steve Brooks took over Allen's outfit, still passengered by Jim, and they walked away with the championship that Allen had won in 2004. We also started to help Lincolnshire newcomer, Mick Finnie. Although we struggled to understand his strange accent Mick was a great laugh and rapidly took to sidecar racing. Allen contented himself with an occasional ride, sometimes passengered by Kenny Williams who, with Rolf Biland, had previously won the World Championship. That was some pedigree, but showed the respect that Allen commanded around the paddock. 2005 was interesting in other ways too; we had an offer of major sponsorship for the team. The offer seemed incredible and would cover most, if not all of our costs as the sponsor - who I won't name for reasons that will become obvious - offered to set up a dedicated bank account for us into which he would deposit regular funds. He arranged for Allen, Duncan and myself to be authorised signatories, organising a meeting at his bank in Chester for this to be sorted. We duly met with the sponsor and a bank official and were given papers to sign. Allen, being more worldly-wise than I am, read these carefully, only to discover that deep in the small print there was a clause which said that the three of us were to become responsible for part of the sponsor's company's liabilities! Allen pointed out this *'mistake'* in no uncertain terms and, after an awkward silence, that was the end of the meeting. We had got off lightly, but it perhaps helped us realise that we were better off under our own, if limited, means.

After that the seasons went by with a good deal of success until 2008, when Allen decided to contest the F350 Championship again with experienced passenger Martin Pither in the chair. By now, Steve Brooks had his own very fast outfit, which Allen was preparing, so Allen had to be content most of the time to battle for second place with a quickly improving Mick Finnie, also on an Allen Steele-prepared machine. This resulted in a funny incident in May, when we had a championship round at Oulton Park. Although it is only just down the road from Allen's house, amazingly we had problems getting to and from the circuit. I arrived at Allen's to find him loading the outfit onto a trailer instead of into the back of our trusty transporter. The problem was not big and mechanical however, it was very small, but also insurmountable. Allen had discovered that a wren had made a nest in the chassis and was raising a brood of noisy chicks. There was no way that Allen would disturb the nest; he'd rather have missed the race. So this is why we started a strange journey to the circuit, with the outfit facing backwards on the trailer, with me sitting on it, holding the brakes on, so it didn't roll off! But it got stranger. We drove back to Allen's to collect the spares only to find a dumbfounded Paul Dumbill there, another friend. He told us that he had gone to the Red Lion pub in the village, where Mick Finnie lived at the time and, as agreed, began to tow Mick on his outfit to the circuit. When he got to Oulton Park however, he discovered the outfit was gone and that when he had retraced his steps, there was no Mick Finnie, or outfit, located. We didn't know what to do, but when we finally arrived at the circuit there was Mick calmly waiting for *us*.

He told us in very colourful language that Paul had set off at such a pace that he couldn't keep hold of the tow rope, as that's how they – probably illegally – had planned to make their journey. Stranded at the side of the road, Mick did the only thing that he could; he bump started the outfit and drove it to the circuit under its own steam. The story could have ended there but after the meeting the owner needed their trailer back. As such Allen decided to do what Mick Finnie had attempted, towing his outfit by rope behind a car driven by Duncan, our retired police friend. Allen steered whilst I sat in the chair, gripping the rope tightly. We got a few strange looks as we passed through villages on our way, but our slow and steady trip was otherwise uneventful. We had just turned into Allen's gate and closed it behind us when we saw a police car drive past however. Someone had obviously heard a noisy outfit on the quiet country road and had reported it. Thankfully, the coppers missed us as Duncan, being a recently retired policeman, would have had some explaining to do. But what of the noisy sidecar I hear you ask? Oh, that was Mick Finnie's. He simply rode his outfit home. He was quite a character, but unfortunately not with us for very long. During the winter he was diagnosed with a brain tumour and in June I got the inevitable phone call. It was hard to believe that the likeable, larger-than-life character would no longer be at the meetings with us and many of the sidecar

Allen with ex-World Champion Kenny Williams, with whom he'd sometimes race

racing fraternity turned up for Mick's memorial service. Afterwards, we took his ashes to scatter at Oulton Park where - strictly against circuit instructions - someone climbed over the fence at Cascades and scattered Mick's remains over the track. After a solemn moment, one of the assembled group quipped, *'That's the first time he's ever been on the right line!'* and everyone erupted into laughter, just how Mick would have wanted it.

The 2009 season was a very similar affair, but with Paul Owen from Stoke-on-Trent becoming a regular podium finisher. Allen prepared Paul's engine, along with his own and that of Steve Brooks, thereby ensuring that he had fast, reliable competition. Steve was again dominant throughout the season, but Allen and Paul were there to fight over the win if he had any problems and it resulted in the season finishing with Steve Brooks winning the championship, Allen coming second and Paul Owen in third. This meant that engines prepared by Allen had finished in the top three places in the series. It was a great advert for his engine preparation skills which was important as BSK Racing would be involved with the series for a few seasons yet. Other drivers were piloting our outfit now but Allen prepared the engines and I was writing race reports for the FSRA magazine amongst others. Through this I heard that Allen was to be awarded an unspecified trophy at the presentation in November 2012 and I was tasked to persuade him to attend. I told Allen that I was planning to go and, if he wanted, I could give him a lift: thankfully, he agreed. At the dinner, we had a chat with TT winner John Holden who was - unsurprisingly for a sidecar driver - very down to earth and by a process of elimination, I worked out that the trophy that would be awarded to Allen was the Mick Finnie Trophy. This trophy, in memory of our friend, was for the person who had contributed greatest to the race series, with the recipient being voted for by all of the other sidecar racing teams.

I was pleased to hear Allen's name read out, but was surprised to hear that he was the joint winner; *I* was the other half. The riders and passengers were rewarding us for being prepared to help anyone and everyone in the paddock. Allen and I looked at each other and I don't know who was more shocked. We went up to receive the trophy from the guest of honour, Stan Dibben, who was the World Sidecar Championship-winning passenger to Eric Oliver in 1953, the year that I was born. What an end to the season.

As it happened, 2013 was a mixed season for the team and by the end of it we all knew that the time had come to wind-up our sidecar racing. The work and cost was proving too much for Allen, but BSK wasn't quite over yet. In 2015 Allen and myself were invited over to the Isle of Man for the 60th anniversary of the first Southern 100 races. It was a great affair and I think acted as a spur, as Allen and I didn't feel that we could just leave racing altogether. We started by preparing an air-cooled Yamaha 250 and eventually persuaded Rob Knight to make a low-key racing comeback, by riding in the Tonfanau Classic Championship, Tonfanau being a small circuit in Wales. Rob took to the bike very well, but we had several frustrating meetings so, at the end of the season, it was decided to invest in the parts to run the bike as a 350cc the following year instead. The required cylinder-heads were located at Padgett's of Batley and I was dispatched to collect them.

Allen had told me to ask for Clive Padgett specifically on arrival, though I was a little nervous about approaching one of the most successful sponsors in the history of Isle of Man racing over such trifling little parts. After all, Clive had been the brains behind Ian Hutchinson's unrepeatable five TT wins in a week and had backed many of the most recent stars in road racing, including Kiwi Bruce Anstey. I needn't have worried. When I introduced myself, Clive sat me down, got me a cup of tea and proceeded to ask about my involvement with Allen over the years. Even after this short chat, Clive told me that he considered me to be a friend and that I was welcome to visit him any time. Of course, Allen's long association with the Padgett's dynasty was the key to Clive's door, but even so, as a complete stranger, Clive gave me a very warm and sincere welcome. I was to re-visit Padgett's several times over the next few years collecting more Yamaha parts and every time, no matter how busy he was, Clive would get me a cup of tea and have a chat about how we were getting along: a true enthusiast.

Allen doing what he did, and still does, best. Working on a two-stroke engine

With the bike equipped with Clive's bits, Rob started to become more and more competitive. He was rarely out of the first three and we all enjoyed our weekends. Eventually, with 350 numbers dwindling, we decided to convert the bike back to a 250 again, so that Rob could face sterner competition. He did, but signed off his racing career by winning the 2022 championship.

With Rob retired the Yamaha is now sitting in Allen's garage, but with no one lined-up to ride, is that the end? I don't know, but it's not the most important question anyway. Apart from asking Steff to marry me - which she denies I ever did - the most important question was always the one I asked back in 1973, *'Why doesn't this newspaper have a motorcycling column?'* It shaped my life in so many ways, none to be forgotten.

Acknowledgements

I'd like to thank everyone mentioned in this book for being involved in my motorcycling journey one way or another. However, there have been many more who have played a part and deserve my thanks. This alphabetical list will have to serve and I apologise to anyone who has been omitted. Here goes:- Mark Aisbett, Jeff Baines, Mal Barrow, Steve Bradbury, John Bywater, Dennis Calvert, Kevin Chandler, Don & Jean Clayton, Ian Crank, Pat Crawford, Max Crosland, Pat Dolan, Colin Downing, Trevor Downing, Alan Edwards, Dave Green, Martin & Karen Hamer, John Hammond, Vicky Hilton, Phil & Cindy Howard, Bill Jackson, Nick Jeffery, Gordon & Julie Jones, Patrycja Kostolowska, John Lockett, Alex Luti, Jim McFarlane, Dudley Martin, Ralph & Joy Martin, Al Melling, Keith Mellor, Kevin Moore, John Phelan, Steve Rigby, Paul Rhodes, Dave Robinson, John Steele, Konrad Strycharz, Paul Tetlow, Ian Thompson, Dave Tibbles, Chris Tindall, Tim Walker, Frank Westworth, Chris Wright and Steve Wrigley.

Also, I'd like to thank those motorcycle writers and journalists who have inspired me over the years. I can never hope to write with such skill so my admiration for their work knows no bounds; Peter Egan (Cycle World), Dave Minton (Motorcycle Sport, Motor Cycle Illustrated etc.), Ray Knight (Motor Cycle Illustrated), Ted Simon (Jupiter's Travels) and Robert Pirsig (Zen and the Art of Motorcycle Maintenance).

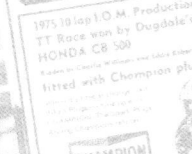